Contents

Introduction

OONAGH HARTNETT, GILL BODEN,
and MARY FULLER*

Feminism questions accepted conceptualizations about the sexes. As a result of this challenge from the Women's Movement, research on sex differences and sex roles is beginning to acquire new meanings within psychology. Feminist perspectives promise to do more than just extend existing frames of reference but rather to provide qualitatively different ones, and in so doing to contribute to greater intellectual rigour. Analysis of sex roles and sex stereotyping may be capable of advancing our insights into the human condition as a whole, into our modes of thinking and categorizing, into our attitudes and values, and into our ways of acting. In fact, just as much as the analysis of many other variables that we would not think of ignoring – variables such as individual differences, class, race, level of technology, and so on – can do. (This argument is more fully discussed in the Afterword.) For these reasons the study of sex roles and sex stereotyping is shifting from a peripheral to a more central position in the

*The editors' names are given in random order.

research endeavours of psychologists.

Against this background it was decided to call a conference to bring together researchers actively interested in these concerns, particularly those working in Western Europe, to provide an overview of their hitherto isolated efforts. In the summer of 1977 an international conference was held in the Department of Applied Psychology, UWIST, Cardiff under the auspices of the British Psychological Society (Welsh Branch). This book arises from that conference.

In selecting papers for inclusion we were guided by the desire to provide an alternative to the mainly American studies that have so far been available. We have aimed to bring together, in an easily accessible form, a collection of studies that gives some indication of the ideas, issues, problems, and methods with which British researchers in this field are concerning themselves. Nine of the papers are written by British researchers and/or concern Britain; one is from France, another from Belgium, and two from the United States of America. Three of these were selected because their subject-matter complements that being discussed by their British colleagues, while Ruth Ekstrom's has no British counterpart, being concerned with action-oriented research. Ekstrom discusses the practical implications of integrating research with the implementation of public policy and social change, as distinct from being a theoretical discussion of this goal as an ideal.

The papers represent a variety of approaches. These include historical surveys, critiques of previous research, theoretical speculations, and recently conducted empirical studies. To some extent nearly all the papers employ a mixture of approaches.

The first three papers in this collection together constitute an overview of research into the field of sex differences and sex-role stereotyping. The paper by Esther Saraga and Dorothy Griffiths concentrates on the research into cognitive abilities. It considers the assumptions underlying this area of research, the methodology, and wider social and political implications. The authors suggest that the effect of much of this research is to reinforce the *status quo*, and they argue strongly that, instead of looking for the source of such differences in biological or genetic arguments, a more valuable approach would be one that stressed the uniqueness of human beings in their capacities for choice and the creation of their own history.

Janet Sayers, in her paper, raises the question of the measurement of masculinity and femininity, and their relation to behavioural sex differences. She disputes their possible origin in the reproductive division of labour between the sexes. She criticizes the measures that have been used partly because they ignore the unconscious and less-often articulated contradictions in people's ideas about the differences between the sexes. This is a point central to John Rowan's contribution in which he discusses the development of masculine identity in terms of its relation to the dichotomous view of women implicit in our cultural stereotype. He considers the comparatively rarely discussed detrimental effects that sex-role stereotyping may have on men.

The second section contains three papers that focus on motherhood and, more particularly, on the active cognitive attribution of meaning that women bring to their experience of motherhood. The first two papers provide evidence that the feelings and attitudes women have towards motherhood may be ambiguous or ambivalent despite the fact that being a parent has long been taken for granted as the most fulfilling activity for women.

Haydée Marcos explores the prospective mother's perceptions of her relationship with her own parents, the place of motherhood in her life, and her image of the expected child. She concludes that the mother's feelings of self-worth as an individual and as a woman appear to be central. Marcos also points out the importance of the mother's relationship with her own father in shaping her feelings of self-worth.

Eva Zajicek's paper also addresses the theme of self-worth with an exploration of the correlation between low self-esteem in women and problems during pregnancy and early motherhood.

Janet Berson adopts a similar approach to that of the two previous papers, in that she too is interested in the way people define their own situations. In her work she considers the costs that a woman perceives will be incurred in combining career and family roles. She examines the trade-offs in which young women feel that a choice of career will involve them when this is combined with motherhood. Women in her sample, whether married or single, with or without children, all valued highly personal independence, feelings of self-worth, and care of children. This agreement also held true for those aspects of life that were negatively valued, namely, threats to the marriage and having other people to care for one's children. The women perceived beneficial effects from having a career outside the home in terms of an increase in autonomy or personal independence, but also saw the likelihood of increased threats to their marriages.

Papers in the next section consider attitudes towards success and failure and the conditions under which either or both may be feared or desired. The results of some previous empirical studies indicate that fear of success may particularly affect women and girls. Colleen Ward is critical of many of the previous studies in the area of fear of success. In this context she discusses the expectancy-value theory of motivation. Nicole Viaene's paper which follows presents a study of sex differences in causal attributions for success and failure. Results indicated 'that girls attributed their success more to luck and less to ability than boys; they also tended to show more luck attributions for failure'. However these sex differences in attributions could not be explained by sex differences in initial expectation of success.

Part five deals with the effect of sex-role stereotyping in education. Roger Murphy gives data on sex differences in examination performance in Britain. He rejects any simple theory of innate sex differences in ability which may be used to account for sex differences in examination performance. His data show a significantly larger number of boys than girls entering for O level examinations in science subjects and Helen Weinreich-Haste in the next paper attempts to show why this should be the case. She suggests that science is only a particular example of a more general typification of most branches of knowledge as 'masculine' and that subjects commonly thought of as 'feminine' are in fact often merely perceived as 'less masculine'. She argues convincingly that this typification must have an inhibiting effect on girls' choice of subject and performance, and concludes that knowledge needs 'desexing'.

Part six has been given the title 'Androgyny' – a concept that has gained ground recently. This term is used to describe what is seen to be a potentially valuable cluster of personality traits and psychological attributes that combine both stereotypically masculine and feminine qualities and thus render a person situationally more effective.

David Hargreaves' study of creativity in children starts from the standpoint that 'sex-typed response styles are by no means unmodifiable psychological characteristics' and concludes that for the children in his study 'our manipulation of response styles on a cognitive test operates mainly on a level of adoption in that sex-roles are consciously being enacted rather than unconsciously internalized in any sense'.

Jenny Williams shows a relationship between levels of both masculine and feminine characteristics and indices of mental health. She relates the higher mental health scores of high androgyny people to a greater ability on their part to respond more flexibly and appropriately to different situations and thus control and create their environment.

Ruth Ekstrom, in the final section, provides a brief introduction to the thinking behind conscious and systematic attempts to reduce sex-role stereotyping in many areas of the school curriculum and organization. She describes several programmes currently operating in the USA and stresses the careful preparation that needs to take place before intervention strategies can be effective. This preparation involves a recognition of the fact that schools do not exist in a social vacuum and therefore that schemes to reduce prejudice and discrimination based on sex cannot be located solely in educational institutions but need to operate on a broad front encompassing parents, educational administrators, and the community in general, if changes are to have any hope of lasting. Ekstrom also emphasizes the need to carry out follow-up and evaluation studies.

Although the papers in this book have different starting points certain common themes emerge, in particular the distinction between male and masculine and female and feminine – that is between sex and gender, between that which is biologically determined and that which is assigned and therefore, theoretically at least, amenable to change.

Several authors explicitly refer to the notion of psychological androgyny, the capacity possessed by certain individuals of combining high levels of both stereotypically masculine and feminine characteristics. Helen Weinreich-Haste, with apparent paradox, states that, 'creative male scientists get to the top by expression of their masculine personalities but their creativity comes from a non-masculine way of thinking', and other authors while not necessarily using the term 'androgyny' suggest that greater flexibility of behaviour could bring rewards. Rowan, for instance, discusses the damaging effects of the male role in terms of the concept of psychic celibacy, 'an internal mechanism by means of which each person cuts themselves off from part of their own reality' (i.e. their cross-sex characteristics) that 'would need to be broken down if men and women were to reveal their potential and avoid being limited or crippled'.

Marcos and Zajicek, in the section on motherhood, suggest that the whole-hearted acceptance of the feminine role may not be the best strategy for women in coping with being a mother. Sayers, commenting on some of the contradictory data and theory on the fit between psychological femininity and maternal adjustment, concludes that, 'some so-called feminine traits are not only not relevant but are maladapted for maternity'. Rowan, Hargreaves, and Weinreich-Haste in particular also highlight the possibly inhibiting effects of the sex-role stereotypes upon men.

A related theme is the consideration of levels of achievement in women. The papers on fear of success, examination results, and areas of knowledge can all be said to support the view that sex-stereotyping has detrimental effects on women's achievement as well as on the advancement of knowledge and the fostering of creativity in general.

The need for women to have a sense of positive self-worth, autonomy, and independence, which is often thought of as a stereotypically masculine attribute, is reiterated throughout this collection of papers. It arises in connection with mental health and the avoidance of stress, as well as with coping with unavoidable stress particularly at specific crisis points in life.

Another theme brought out more or less implicitly by a number of authors is the importance of considering the environmental, cultural, and structural factors affecting the role of the sexes. They are particularly critical of limiting the basis of explanation to biological factors. The study of sex differences that takes all these factors into account has its uses at a practical level, for example, in the devising of programmes aimed at compensating for the effects of past discrimination on skill levels and work experience or in the design of equipment, technology, and work systems that can comfortably be used and operated by both women and men. Saraga and Griffiths also stress the importance of the social and political context in which psychological research is undertaken and its findings utilized. An action-oriented approach implying a symbiotic relationship between pure and applied research is a perspective common to a number of papers. Rowan defines as a problem his own role as researcher in

12

interaction with his subjects of study and suggests that research into sex roles is indivisible from personal change in both researcher and researched, while Ekstrom describes the role of the researcher actively involved in systematic change within institutions.

A perspective emerges from these and other papers on the need to take people into account as active participants in their own destiny, in other words to explore the meanings with which people invest their own actions and those of others.

We have not attempted to stamp this book with a particular perspective, nor to push individual papers into one mould. We have confined our editing to attempting to improve clarity and presentation. Nevertheless, many of the perspectives and ideas that emerged at the conference and which the present papers exemplify are those that feminists have espoused for some time.

Acknowledgements

The editors are grateful to Barbara Thomas and Judy Keeney for typing the manuscript.

Oonagh Hartnett would like to thank the Ford Foundation for funding study leave during part of which she co-edited this book.

13

PART ONE

Overviews

ONE

Sex differences in cognitive abilities: a sterile field of enquiry?

DOROTHY GRIFFITHS and ESTHER SARAGA

During the last decade there has been a significant increase in research in the social sciences on sex differences, sex role development and stereotyping, and related areas.[1] Much of this research has been simply descriptive in nature but where explanations have been sought they have been primarily within a biological framework. In this paper we shall present a brief overview of research in one such area – sex differences in cognitive abilities – and shall argue that it should be evaluated not only in its own terms, as is conventional, but also as a social product of a particular set of historical circumstances.

Our approach will be to argue, first, that since psychological research does not exist in total isolation from society, it must be considered as a social product, and it is therefore important to analyse the assumptions upon which both the construction of its theories and methodologies are based; second, that psychological knowledge is a form of knowledge – scientific knowledge – which

17

has a particularly central status in contemporary society, and this status affects both the presentation of, and the response to, its findings and conclusions in important ways; third, that an examination of the specific historical conditions under which research in this area has been of particular interest is helpful for understanding its ideological dimensions. This paper will argue that examination from this broader perspective casts serious doubts on the intellectual value of the research.

Sex differences in cognitive abilities: contemporary research

Contemporary research can be divided into two strands: studies that attempt to document differences and studies concerned with their explanation. The former consist of little more than a series of *ad hoc* empirical studies in which the choice of behaviour under study often appears to be arbitrary. For many of these researchers, sex, once a 'nuisance' to be controlled for in any study, has now become an essential independent variable. In the latter, the emphasis on biologically-based explanations is justified by reference to human evolutionary history. It is argued that the biological division of labour for reproduction structures the social division of labour between the sexes. Cognitive ability differences are a consequence of the former and are thus reflected in the latter.

Detailed accounts of the various temperament and ability differences that have been reported are available elsewhere[2] and little use will be served by our repeating them here. The most widely reported differences in cognitive abilities are the superior performance of women in tests of verbal skills and the superior performance of men in tests of visual-spatial ability and mathematics. These findings have stimulated a variety of biological explanations but while the details of particular theories have been subject to challenge and change, the biological mechanisms upon which they have focussed have remained relatively consistent. There have been three major focal points.

First, both the verbal and spatial differences have been related to differences in the rate, and hence degree of *brain lateralization*, although theorists differ on the details. Thus, Buffery and Gray (1972) explain spatial differences in terms of greater female lateralization whereas Witelson (1976) suggests the opposite argument – that there is earlier and greater lateralization in boys.

18

A second type of explanation suggests that both differences arise from the differential effect of male and female *hormones* (androgens and oestrogens) on brain activity (for example Broverman *et al.* 1968), while a third suggestion is that superior spatial ability in men is *inherited*. Stafford (1961) proposed a sex-linked recessive gene hypothesis, but more recently Bouchard and McGee (1977) have suggested that the data may be compatible with a 'sex-limitation' hypothesis.

Having argued that cognitive ability differences exist, and then proposed a biological mechanism to explain their ontogenetic development, these theories then claim that the differences are consistent with human evolution because these particular traits have adaptive significance and would therefore have been favoured in selection processes during evolution. Hutt (1972), for example, argues that women have superior verbal fluency *because* it was adaptive for the young child to be reared in a rich linguistic environment, while men have superior spatial ability *because* this was adaptive for hunting. Embodied in this argument is thus the idea that traits that were adaptive during evolution have become fixed in the gene pool of the species.

The current social roles of women and men can then be explained in terms of these ability differences, and associated differences in temperament,[3] and justified by reference to a biological and evolutionary base. Again, Hutt (1972) argues that it is *because* women have superior manual dexterity that they become typists or find themselves assembling electronic components. Similarly the scarcity of women architects and engineers is accounted for in terms of women's lack of spatial ability (Coltheart 1975).

This research has aroused more than just academic interest since it clearly has important implications for social policy. And in an era in which many women are challenging the present arrangement of female and male social roles, its conclusion – that there are biological limits to the extent to which change is possible – has made the research contentious among both social scientists and feminists.[4]

The historical context

Neither this area of research nor the controversy surrounding it is new. In the western world, theories about women's biological inferiority date back at least to Hippocrates (c.400B.C.; quoted in O'Faolain and Martines 1973). The immediate origin of today's theories, however, can be traced to the second half of the nineteenth century. Like our own, this was a period characterized by great interest in these questions. There were three main emphases in the research conducted at this time. The first focussed on *brain differences* between the sexes. These differences were originally expressed in terms of differences in phrenology (the study of areas of the brain surface introduced by Gall: see Walker 1850), and later in terms of the size of either the whole brain (see e.g. Bain 1875, Romanes 1887) or of the particular cortical lobe thought to be the site of mental capacities (e.g. Rudinger 1877). All the research claimed to demonstrate the intellectual inferiority of women and it appears that changes in biological and psychological ideas about the brain were followed fairly rapidly by changes in ideas about sex differences in the brain. For example in the 1870s intellectual functions were thought to be sited in the frontal lobes, and men's frontal lobes were said to be larger than women's (Rudinger 1877). By the end of the century, ideas about the site of the intellect had changed, and it was thought to be located in the parietal lobes. Parallel developments are found in the sex-differences literature. Thus, Patrick (1895), one of the researchers in this field, wrote

'the frontal region is not as has been supposed smaller in women, but rather larger relatively . . . But the parietal lobe is somewhat smaller, [furthermore] a preponderance of the frontal region does not imply intellectual superiority . . . the parietal region is really the most important.' (Quoted in Shields 1975)

A second emphasis concerned the influence of *women's reproductive functions* which were thought to be the cause of a wide variety of 'diseases'.[5] Theories about women's intellectual capacities focussed on the onset of menstruation at puberty and influenced by ideas about the conservation of energy, argued that, for girls, intellectual work during puberty would use up energy that was necessary for the development of reproductive functions. This could have the extreme effect of masculinizing their bodies (1869 review of J.S. Mill in *The Lancet*), and would certainly render them infertile, thus endangering the future of the race (Clarke 1873, Moore 1886).[6]

A third line of argument focussed on the *variability of characteristics* in women and men, arguing that variability was associated with evolutionary progress. Since male characteristics were more variable than those of women, it was not surprising that men achieved more in all spheres. (See, for example, Geddes and Thomson 1889, Ellis 1903). The debate about variability continued well into the twentieth century (e.g. Thorndike 1906, 1910; Hollingworth 1914) and has reappeared in recent research (Heim 1970; Hutt 1974).

These theories were developed in the context of growing demands from middle-class women, both in Britain and the USA, for access to higher education and to the professions. And they were used in arguments against granting women such access presented by serious scientists in major journals such as *The Lancet*.[7] But they did not go unopposed: Elizabeth Garrett Anderson (1874), for example, fought back at the medical establishment and countered the medical arguments in their own terms. More generally as women gradually gained access to education the opponents of these theories could argue not only that women were intellectually capable of higher education, but that they showed few signs of intellectual damage as a result of it. (Other critics of these theories included: Mill (1869); Duffey (1874); Howe (1874); Bebel (1879); Pfeiffer (1888); McClaren (1880-90).)

Reviewing this whole area of research, Helen Thompson Woolley (1910:310) suggested that, 'There is perhaps no field aspiring to be scientific where flagrant personal bias, logic martyred in the cause of supporting a prejudice, unfounded assertions and even sentimental rot and drivel, have run riot to such an extent as here.' By this time the general opinion was that there were few, if any, sex differences in intellect that were of biological origin (although there was still a strong belief in the biological basis of emotional differences). But as Woolley (1910) pointed out this did not mean that the opposition to women's entry into higher education or the professions had waned, but merely that the content of the argument had had to change.

'The cry is no longer that woman will injure herself by the mental and physical over-strain involved in the higher intellectual training, but that she will injure society by reducing her own reproductive activity (later marriages, fewer marriages, fewer children, opposition between intellectual and sexual functions), and thus lessen the chances of the best element to perpetuate itself.' (Woolley 1910: 342)

Nineteenth and twentieth–century parallels

Although the debate about sex differences in cognitive abilities appears to have died down after the First World War, there has clearly been a resurgence of such ideas in the last ten years, and it is useful to compare the more recent theories with those of the earlier period. Although most of the nineteenth-century scientists sought to demonstrate women's intellectual *inferiority*, some, for example Geddes and Thomson (1889), preferred to discuss the 'complementarity' of the sexes. Today, when few dare suggest explicitly that women are *inferior* to men, such arguments about complementarity are very common. It is claimed that since women and men have different kinds of ability, they should be regarded as 'equal but different'. Implicitly, however, a lower evaluation of female ability is still being made, and this becomes clear once the reader has penetrated the mystifying jargon in which the conclusions are frequently expressed. The work of Broverman *et al.* provides a good example of this. They characterize the skills at which women excel as involving 'minimal mediation by higher cognitive processes' whereas those at which men excel are said to involve 'extensive mediation of higher processes' (Broverman *et al.* 1968:28). Today no-one is using these arguments in order to exclude women from higher education *per se*. Instead they are used to explain and justify their lower representation in higher education and their relative absence from certain areas of work (such as science and engineering).

Nevertheless there are several respects in which there seem to be clear parallels between the nineteenth- and twentieth-century debates in this area. In both periods, broader social and economic changes gave rise to feminist movements making militant demands; in both periods psychological research focussed on biologically based explanations of sex differences in intellectual ability; and, finally, in both periods, these arguments have been used (implicitly or explicitly) to support the continuation of a social system that is oppressive to women. Much of the research has pointed, more or less strongly, to the long-term futility of feminist demands. The nineteenth-century research

22

suggested initially that women were incapable of higher education, and later that it would result in adverse physical consequences. Contemporary research, more subtly, does not deny that changes are possible but indicates that there are limits to them. Hutt for example argues, 'Thus, the very psychological dispositions of women appear to militate against great achievements in competitive fields' (Hutt 1972:121).[10]

Such arguments have had and still have the effect of defusing the political demands that women are making by shifting the debate from the political to the biological arena. Political challenges to biological certainties can promise little.

In drawing these parallels we are pointing to the impossibility of evaluating this area of research without considering it in its historical context. Like all science, research on sex differences in cognitive abilities has not developed via an inherent stimulus and logic. Quite the contrary, interest in this area has been greatest in periods characterized by concern with the position of women, and its theoretical developments have been directly related to the demands that women were, or are, making. To say this is not to suggest either a simple determinist or conspiratorial account of the development of the research, or that the topic has been ignored at all other times. Rather, it is to suggest that the social and political environment directs the attention of both researchers and funding agencies to particular questions. In this case the demands that women are making have rendered the question of sex differences more problematic and therefore more research worthy.[11]

The failure by most commentators to consider the research in its historical context means that their reviews stop after an evaluation of the research in its own terms. Two important and related issues are thus ignored. The first concerns the utility of the biological paradigm in explaining human behaviour and attributes; the second asks why a biological paradigm has been used so consistently in this and other related areas of research, during the last 100 years.[12] Before discussing these questions ourselves we must also consider the research in its own terms.[13]

The research in its own terms

We stated earlier that it is difficult to summarize the empirical evidence for sex differences in cognitive abilities. Two recent reviews by Maccoby and Jacklin (1974) and Fairweather (1976) both suggest that there is very little evidence of cognitive-ability differences before puberty. Maccoby and Jacklin claim that the only reliably observed differences are female superiority in language skills and male superiority in mathematics and visual-spatial skills. But Block (1976) has criticized their method of simply counting the number of studies reporting a particular result, and their criteria for accepting a sex difference as established, and has claimed that as a consequence they have omitted positive findings. Fairweather, however, considered the studies concerned with spatial and linguistic skills in detail and still concluded that there was very little evidence of differences. 'Certainly, the incidence of such differences is outnumbered by the qualifications noted in the present review: age; culture; birth order; family size; sex of experimenter; and replicability both between and within studies' (Fairweather 1976:266). Biological explanations seem to have taken little note of such reviews. Yet the lack of reliably observed differences before puberty must cause difficulties, for example, for theories that are expressed in terms of brain lateralization, because other differences associated with lateralization are certainly found by the age of six years (Fairweather 1976; Witelson 1976).

We have already pointed out, too, that many of the studies appear to be *ad hoc* empirical investigations of a chosen sex difference. Thus the belief that it is possible to describe 'what is' without reference to a theoretical framework is either implicit in many investigations, or, as for Maccoby and Jacklin, made an explicit starting point. The data produced by these investigations are purportedly free of theoretical assumptions, and theories 'emerge' via *post hoc* theorization. Several problems arise from this research strategy.

First, the principle of neutral observation is in itself dubious. Observer and observed cannot be separated as clearly and as easily as many researchers suggest. Observations are always structured in some way by theory, and the very belief that they need not be is a theoretical position. Researchers do not approach an experiment or observation cold, experiments are conducted to test an idea, and observations are made with reference to something. This point is important but is rarely recognized in psychology. Scientific theory is neither discovered nor does it emerge from the 'facts': it is produced and the ways in which experiments are set up and the subjects of observations established are related to the social and historical context in which they are conducted.[14] This must, in turn, cast doubt on a second and related assumption that individuals can be abstracted from their environment and observed without reference to this broader social world. In common with much of psychology, research on cognitive ability differences assumes that human beings have an 'essential nature' that is independent of their social environment, and which may be discovered through observation and experiment. Such a static conception of human nature ignores not only historical and cross-cultural variations but also developmental processes, and leads all too easily to biologically based explanations.[15]

An example here may both clarify our argument and show its relevance to the research that we are discussing. The field of research we are considering is concerned with sex *differences*.[16] Since the focus of interest is on differences rather than similarities, it is the former that are observed, reported, and theorized, while the latter are ignored. The focus on differences means that the very considerable overlaps in the distributions of the scores of the two sexes on various tests are rarely reported. As Maccoby and Jacklin (1974) point out, this bias of interest in favour of differences is increased in experimental work through the procedure of testing the null hypothesis, which has the effect of rendering findings of no difference uninteresting, unlikely to be written up, and even more unlikely to be published.

As a result of this bias, which is systematic, occurring in almost all studies, there is an extensive literature on differences between the sexes and a very small literature on similarities. Obviously this has important implications for theory which is also developed to explain *differences*. And, as we suggested in the last section, this focus on differences is not the outcome of some logic inherent in the science. Like the variation in interest at different historical times, the focus on differences can also be related to the broader social and historical context.

Another major problem in the research concerns the use of the concept of 'ability'. Like the concept of 'intelligence' it implies the existence in the brain of some capacity that is either of fixed quantity, or can vary only within a fairly limited range. It is assumed both that it can be measured and that individual differences can be expressed in a quantitative form. This conception of intellectual performance is completely out of date within psychology itself. Current views of the brain refer, instead, to different kinds of information *processing*; that is, they involve a non-static conception of performance that may well not be readily measurable on a linear scale. In sex-differences research, specific abilities are inferred from performance on particular tasks, yet little consideration is given to analysing the information processing requirements of the tasks (even within the current limits of our ability to do this). As a result, a whole range of tasks have been used in different studies claiming to measure the same ability.[17] Furthermore, it is generally assumed that different subjects will approach the same task in the same way, thus ignoring the very real probability that it may be executed in different ways by different people. For example, a task described as spatial may sometimes be carried out verbally, and vice versa (Marshall 1973, Coltheart *et al.* 1975). In addition, in assuming that performance on a task is a direct measure of a specific ability, factors such as anxiety, motivation, and expectations, which are known to affect performance differentially between the sexes, are completely ignored.

These problems are compounded when comparisons are made between the performances of animals and humans. In many cases a biological explanation for a human sex difference is supported by the claim that the same difference is found in animals (Broverman *et al.*1968:27, Buffery and Gray 1972:123).[18] Implicit in such arguments is the assumption that the same 'ability' has been studied in each case. In rats spatial ability is usually measured by their performance in mazes. Humans, however, are not tested in the maze at Hampton Court, instead our performance is often measured by tasks requiring the mental manipulation of objects. Yet there is no evidence that these tasks involve comparable cognitive processes. Such comparisons with animal studies should therefore be used with extreme caution.

Unfortunately they frequently provide the basis for overly simple biological explanations of fairly complex social phenomena. A particularly clear example of this is found in Hutt's book *Males and Females*,[19] in which she suggests that greater male achievement is related to their greater persistence and singlemindedness, and that this in turn is caused by their higher levels of testosterone (male hormone). Evidence for this conclusion, though, is actually derived from studies of *chicks*. Thus Hutt's explanation of greater male achievement in the human depends upon two assumptions: that legitimate conclusions can be drawn from studies of animals; and that there is a simple cause-effect link between hormones and behaviour. Neither assumption is either made explicit or justified. In particular she gives no indication at all that she is reporting animal studies, and only the curious or dedicated reader with access to academic journals will follow up the references and discover this.

Another difficulty concerns the ease with which extrapolations are made from reports of sex differences to explanations of social roles. Earlier we pointed out that sex differences in social role, and particularly in patterns of employment, are often explained in terms of differences in cognitive abilities. But the considerable overlap in the distributions of test scores renders such explanations extremely doubtful. The low representation of women in engineering, for example, is often attributed to women's poor performance on tests of spatial ability. Yet Kelly (1974) has estimated that if entry into engineering depended on spatial ability alone, then the ratio of women to men would be 2:3. In the UK the ratio is currently more like 1:100.

These simple extrapolations from ability to social role ignore the vast range of social, psychological, and economic factors that affect, in this case, choice of employment. Moreover when 'social influences' are considered they are treated as purely external factors, and considered in terms of the differential treatment of the sexes. Consequently, the finding that, even where there is apparently no differential treatment, sex differences may nevertheless emerge is taken as strong evidence of biological determination.[20] This kind of argument ignores the importance of the internalization of social experiences and the development of gender identity as critical factors influencing an individual's expectations about her/his future role. Thus, for example, Torrance (1963) found that even when girls had performed as well as boys on a science test, both sexes still thought that the boys had done better.[21]

Taken together the comments in this section constitute a serious critique of the research. The response of many researchers to such criticisms is to accept that much of the research has been 'bad science' while ignoring the importance of evaluating it within a broader framework. Thus their response is to try to produce 'better' science without challenging the existing framework. Ours, in comparison, it to examine the relevance and utility of this framework itself.

The biological paradigm

In a society in which women and men have different and unequal social roles we would expect certain psychological sex differences to develop. As we have shown the extent of these differences has been exaggerated and some of this exaggeration may well follow from the theoretical framework used to explain them.

The biological paradigm is both very influential and widely accepted as a framework for the explanation of human social behaviour, yet its underlying assumptions are rarely analysed. One of the most important of these is that *conclusions about human behaviour may be drawn from studies of animal behaviour*. This is dependent upon an implicit, but nevertheless strong emphasis on continuities between humans and other species – an emphasis that is, in its turn, justified by appeals to our common evolutionary heritage. While not denying that human beings are animals, nor that there are consequent continuities, for example in certain physiological processes, we believe that such an exclusive focus on continuities means that the potential significance of the discontinuities that exist in behaviour and attributes is not adequately considered. When these are considered important doubts about the value of such extrapolations are raised.

Human beings are different from other animals in several respects. First, the importance of learning increases as the evolutionary scale is ascended, and humans learn a much higher proportion of their behaviour than any other species. While the human infant is genetically predisposed to develop certain forms of behaviour (language, social interaction, and so on), the detailed content of that behaviour will depend upon the social environment in which the infant develops. The richness and diversity of human behaviour, as illustrated by cross-cultural and historical data, is evidence of the extent of this learning.

Second, humans have a far more complex system of verbal communication than even the closest primates, and abilities developed by this have been amplified through the written and printed word. In particular humans have developed complex

28

systems of cultural transmission that enable knowledge to be passed on between generations on a scale and complexity that no primate species approaches.

Third, and related to this, human beings are able to manipulate their environment on a scale unparalleled in other species. Remarkable though the hive or ants' nest may be, and the organization by which they were created – in what sense can they be regarded as equivalent to the physical infrastructure of a twentieth-century city? The interaction of humans with their physical environment, and their ability to intervene in it, to improve agricultural yields, for example, is quite unlike that of other species.

Fourth, unlike other species, we can separate the conception of a task from its execution. As Marx said,

> 'A spider conducts operations that resemble those of a weaver, and a bee puts to shame many an architect in the construction of her cells. But what distinguishes the best of bees from the worst of architects is this, that the architect raises his structure in his imagination before he erects it in reality. At the end of every labour process, we get a result that already existed in the imagination of the labourer at its commencement.' (Marx 1954:174)

In other words human beings act with conscious intent and, unlike other species, are able significantly to change the way in which particular tasks are carried out, as is evidenced by, for example, the transformation of craft skills into the monotony of the assembly line.

Finally, and perhaps most importantly, we can create our own history. Most of us spend most of our lives failing to recognize this, and the dominant ideology of our society encourages us to believe that the social order is not only legitimate but also 'natural', and hence inevitable and not open to change. Biologically based explanations of human social behaviour provide an important input into this ideology. However it is difficult to reconcile this model of social change with the record of human history. How, for example, can a biologically based explanation account for very rapid social change such as the events of the Chinese Revolution? These events can only be explained as the self-conscious acts of human beings.

As the vast literature on, for example, the social organization and modes of communication of other animals testifies, the qualities that we have mentioned are not uniquely human (Brown 1965; Box 1973; Argyle and Cook 1976); nevertheless it is our view that each of these characteristics is sufficiently developed in humans to constitute an order of magnitude difference from other animals, a difference that if accepted, constitutes a definitive challenge to the legitimacy of animal-human extrapolation in the context of understanding social behaviour.

A second major assumption of the biological paradigm is that of *evolutionary determinism*. It is assumed not only that human social behaviour has a biological basis, but, further, that it is a manifestation of traits that were fixed during evolution.

In terms of biological as opposed to social evolution, humans must still be considered as a hunter-gatherer species and, as we described earlier, Hutt and others have argued that there is a direct link between superior verbal ability and spatial ability on the one hand, and the child-rearing and hunting roles of women and men respectively on the other. Other researchers have attempted to link different aspects of the contemporary social behaviour of humans with our evolutionary heritage. Tiger (1969), for example, explains the present male dominance in politics through the concept of 'male bonding'. He argues that the successful men in hunter-gatherer societies were those who learned to hunt co-operatively, but that women did not have selection pressures of this kind acting upon them. Thus in politics, and in all other co-operative human activities, both historically and currently, men predominate. Implicit in these arguments is the view that what is biologically or evolutionarily based is therefore 'right', or 'good', and should continue.

There are several criticisms of this kind of argument. To begin with we have very little concrete knowledge of the social structure and behaviour of humans in hunter-gatherer societies (see e.g. Oakley 1974) and certainly not enough to make statements as authoritatively as Tiger *et al.* do. And, as Sayers points out (in the next paper in this volume) the link between particular traits and roles depends on entirely *post hoc* arguments: that is, it is simply assumed that spatial ability, for example, is adaptive for hunting. It is difficult not to suspect that if women showed superiority in tests of spatial ability, the evolutionary determinists would have found some way of arguing that it was adaptive for child rearing. In addition, there is a complete neglect of the potential significance of processes of *social* evolution. The environment in which we now live is clearly very different from that to which we are adapted in biological/evolutionary terms (see, for example, Slater 1977). It is quite possible that aspects of human social behaviour could be evolutionarily adaptive, but that the kinds of environmental stimuli that triggered particular behaviours in hunter-gatherer societies are simply not present in advanced industrial society. Thus even if we have 'behavioural repertoire' it may be completely irrelevant to our present situation. More importantly, the enormous diversity of human behaviour, coupled with our capacity to learn, is suggestive of selection for plasticity of response rather than for fixed outcomes.

It is clear from these arguments that knowledge about the relationship between an individual's genotype and her/his behaviour is still rudimentary. Yet, it is often assumed that it is not only possible *to separate the effects of biological and social influences*, but also to *quantify* them. In discussing this, it is important to recognize that there are two classes of genetically influenced traits: those that are 'developmental fixities', and those that may be mediated by social factors. For the former, the genetic 'programme' as it works out in development is impervious to environmental mediation. This class, which includes traits such as eye colour in humans, is small and not at issue, for our concern is with the latter class.

It is important to recognize that the interaction of 'nature' and 'nurture' is not a simple one of independent factors operating on the organism. They constantly interact, and in such a way that their relative contributions are inseparable. From the moment of conception, the subject of this interaction, at any point in time, is the outcome of previous interactions. Human beings live in a social situation that is characterized by relations of power, different social roles, and so on. Who and what we are, and how we behave, is the product of our continual and iterative interaction with this environment. We can no more escape our social situation than we can deny that we are biological organisms. It follows from this that crude distinctions between 'biological' and 'environmental' influences on behaviour have little meaning.[22]

These statements may sound a little imprecise, particularly when compared with clear, simple theories of biological determinism, but we do not believe that it is possible at our present level of understanding to make more definitive statements about the origins of particular behaviours.

To claim that sex differences are biologically determined is to make a claim that cannot be justified. Despite enormous advances in the last two decades, molecular biology can tell us virtually nothing about the genetic coding of complex behaviours, or even if such a coding exists. Similarly, the relationship between hormones and behaviour is far too poorly understood for unequivocal statements about causality to be made. And the search for hormonal determinants of behaviour fails to recognize that hormones are but one part of a process in the development of behaviour (see e.g. Rose 1976a).

How useful then, is the biological paradigm in the explanation of human social behaviour? We have considerable reservations about its use while denying neither the existence of sex difference in the performance of certain intellectual tasks, nor that biological processes may be involved in their development. We take issue with the suggestion that they are biologically *determined*, and with the consequences of this suggestion for our understanding of the origins and nature of the present arrangement of social roles. The approach set by biological parameters is sterile: after one hundred years it has yet to produce a definitive argument. What is needed is an alternative framework, and in the next section we offer some preliminary proposals for such a framework.

Towards an alternative framework

Environmental determinism is often assumed to be the only alternative to biological determinism. It is not an acceptable alternative, however, and many of our objections apply to all simple determinist models. Neither do we accept the view that it is a 'bit of both', since we have argued that the 'both' do not exist as separate, or separable, entities. Human behaviour is the product of a biological organism developing in a social context. We must thus seek to understand the influence of biology in the context of understanding sex-role stereotyping, the internalization of gender identity, and, crucially, the basis of the social division of labour between the sexes. In order to do this it is necessary to transgress the traditional boundaries of the academic disciplines of biology, psychology, and sociology. We need to recognize that while we have all been socialized into

32

particular disciplines, these have developed historically, and have no absolute significance.[23]

A precise explanation of the particular sex differences in intellectual performance that have been described in the literature is not possible at this stage, but it should start with a recognition of the following. A baby is assigned a particular gender at birth, and this certainly influences the way in which people respond to it. Within the first two years the child develops an understanding of her/his gender identity, and there is some evidence that this process can occur independently of, or even in oppostion to, biological sex (Money *et al*. 1955;1957). The child's understanding of gender identity will, in turn influence the way s/he perceives the world, her/his pattern of identifications, and so on, and this development will take place in a social world that is premissed upon the existence of the sexual division of labour and hence the different social roles, attributes, and abilities of the two sexes. We believe that the development of differences in intellectual skills at puberty has to be understood in the context of the significance for the adolescent child of becoming an adult woman or man. While important biological changes do occur at puberty their influence will be mediated by the way in which they are interpreted by the individual. The onset of menstruation, for example, not only produces hormonal changes, but signifies to the girl that she is a sexual adult and that she can give birth, both of which are very important for women in our society.[24] In a different society, such developments might have a different or lesser significance.

The little cross-cultural data that is available suggests that the patterning of cognitive abilities described in this paper is not universal, but varies with the patterns of socialization (Berry 1966; Dawson 1967; MacArthur 1967). Even where universalities appear to exist this still does not mean that they are biologically determined. For example, some psychologists (Lynn 1962, Chodorow 1971; 1974) are beginning to investigate the differential psychological consequences for girls and boys of early child care being a female role (since this is no longer regarded by psychologists as a biological necessity; see for example Rutter 1972; Schaffer 1977).[25]

Thus we are suggesting that rather than attempting to describe 'what is' and then subjecting these 'findings' to *post hoc* theorizing, the starting point should be the sexual division of labour. We should begin with a theory that accounts for the different social roles of the sexes, and seek to understand the psychological differences between them from within this framework. The importance of considering how people become people in the context of the society in which they live, and how little is understood of this at a psychological level, will then become apparent. Thus understanding the psychological consequences of this inequality becomes a study in the psychology of oppression.

Sex differences, social policy, and science

Throughout its history, research in this area has had important implications for social policy. We have already indicated the role of the nineteenth-century research in arguments about the entry of women into higher education and the professions. The present research is little different, even though it is cloaked in the more liberal disguise of arguing for different *kinds* of education and employment for women. Both the (then) Department of Employment and Productivity and the Department of Education and Science have financed 'basic' research in this area (Gray and Buffery 1971; Buffery and Gray 1972). The Inner London Education Authority in its pamphlet *Career Opportunities for Girls* makes explicit reference to the work of Hutt,[26] and we have already mentioned the influence of these ideas in discussions of girls and science education. At the Conference at which this paper was presented, Betty Lockwood (Chairman of the Equal Opportunities Commission) pointed out that employers frequently claim that women cannot do certain kinds of jobs, and in this context she referred to the relevance and importance of studies of sex differences.

These examples illustrate rather than explain the importance of biologically based explanations. In order to explain both such influence *per se*, and why it has persisted in the face of repeated challenges, we need to shift our focus to science and the role of scientific explanations.

Scientific knowledge has a special status in our society, and it is important to ask why. It derives partly from the claim to be objective and value-neutral knowledge, as well as from its success in explaining and helping us to manipulate the physical world. There is a widespread image of science as consisting of a body of knowledge and a set of techniques that are neutral, at least in the sense that they do not reflect the particular interests of practitioners or sponsors. In addition, to the non-scientist, science appears as an esoteric, complex, impersonal, and mystifying activity that is cloaked in inaccessible jargon. Together the image and mystique of science grant great power to scientific explanations for these appear to deal with facts untainted by value judgements, in contrast to sociological explanations in which the role of value judgements is popularly recognized. This leads to a deference to scientific expertise and judgement, and strengthens explanations and arguments that are supported by appeals to science.[27]

Biological explanations of sex differences in intellectual performance thus have great appeal. First, they are supported by the authority of science and, second, as we argued earlier, they offer a justification of the social, political, and economic *status quo*. In a context where, as we have seen, the dominant ideology suggests that the social order is natural, biological explanations make it also seem inevitable: political challenges, whether by women, blacks, or the working class, are defused by pointing to their futility in biological terms. And, in addition, such explanations appear to be highly plausible for, since their starting point is the *status quo*, they are also explanations of the world of most people's everyday experience.

We have tried to indicate at several points in this paper how and why this image of science is wrong. What it means in the context of research in this particular area is that, despite the existence of relatively damning critiques, the biological arguments not only survive but currently flourish. More complex sociological explanations, which lack this apparent logic, are easily neglected, yet, as we have also tried to point out, without them we cannot begin to provide answers to the questions raised by sex-differences research.

By way of a conclusion

Many contemporary criticisms (including some by psychologists who claim to be feminist) of the kind of research discussed in this paper do not, in our view, take their analysis far enough. There is a tendency to treat psychology as merely biased against women, without recognizing that this bias is not arbitrary, but rather is implicit in many of the assumptions underlying the research.

35

Sex-role socialization is similarly treated as the 'product of arbitrary social stereotypes' (Maccoby and Jacklin, 1974:21), and this can lead to the neglect of questions concerning the origins of these stereotypes. We believe that they arise from the very different social roles of women and men in our society. These roles, in turn, need to be examined and understood as a product of women's oppression under capitalism.[28] An analysis of social roles and cognitive abilities that begins from this perspective provides a structure and framework for the discussion which is absent if socialization is seen as merely arbitrary. It also provides a clearer and more fruitful understanding of how sex-role stereotypes can be changed. Change is not simply a moral question of persuading enough people that it is a good idea, but a political question of transcending structurally based inequalities through the revolutionary transformation of the social structures in which they are rooted.

We end by re-emphasizing that we do not deny the existence, at the present time in our society, of sex differences in performance of certain cognitive tasks. We do, however, reject biological determinist explanations of them, and believe that such explanations are not only based on incorrect assumptions but that they derive from, and reinforce, the ideology of sexism that permeates this society. Questions concerning the origin and nature of sex differences cannot properly be answered by and in a society that is predicated on their existence. And in a society not premissed on their existence, we feel it unlikely that these issues would be a major concern.

Notes

1 One indication of the rate of increase is the number of entries on 'sex differences' in the subject index of *Psychological Abstracts*. In 1955 there were twenty-three (out of a total of 9,103); in 1965 there were sixty-seven (out of 16,619); in the first six months of 1975 under the heading 'human sex differences' there were 426 entries (out of 12,776).

2 See, for example: Garai and Scheinfeld (1968); Gray and Buffery (1971); Buffery and Gray (1972); Hutt (1972); Maccoby and Jacklin (1974); Fairweather (1976); Lloyd and Archer (1976).

3 Historically there has always been a strong belief in the biological basis of emotional and temperamental differences, even in periods when cognitive differences were thought to be of cultural origin.

Space forces us to limit our discussion to research on sex differences in *cognition*. However, we believe that essentially the same criticisms can be applied to studies and theories of temperamental differences.

4   This research is frequently cited in discussions of the low representation of women in science. Two recent examples are a Conference on 'Girls and Science Education' (1975), and a BBC Radio programme *The Mediocrity of Women* (December 1975).

5   See for example: Rosenberg and Rosenberg (1973); Wood (1973); Haller and Haller (1974); Barker-Benfield (1976).

6   This theory first appeared in the USA in a book *Sex in Education* by Edward Clarke (1873). It was taken up in Britain by Henry Maudsley (1874) in an article, 'Sex in Mind and Education'.

7   For a fuller account of nineteenth-century theories, and how they were used in arguments about the education of women, see for example: Bullough and Voght (1973); Burstyn (1973); Shields (1975); Fee (1976); Alaya (1977).

8   There were, of course, other theories developed during this time which also defined women's roles; in particular psychoanalytic ideas and, after the Second World War, theories about maternal deprivation. There are also some interesting exceptions to the general trend of the theories. Fee (1976) refers to a study of the menstrual cycle carried out *during* World War II that suggested that 'as far as scientific evidence goes, there is no reason why women's reproductive functions should interfere with the performance of social functions'. (Seward 1944)

9   For example, Hutt, concludes 'these several results suggest that, despite equality of opportunity, men and women may forge rather different roles for themselves, socially and psychologically. This should occasion not surprise, but relief'. (Hutt 1972.137). And she suggests that 'It is perhaps time women sought to redefine their roles, placing value and emphasis on their particular talents and skills' (Hutt 1972: 138).

The arguments by the 'sex differences' researchers show clear parallels with the more familiar 'race – IQ' debate, although it is much harder to apply the 'equal but different' hypothesis in the latter case. In developing our critique we have drawn on some of the literature from that debate. See for example: Richardson *et al.* (1972); Kamin (1974); Rose (1976b).

10 Some recent commentators echo the nineteenth-century view that deviation from women's 'natural' role will be biologically disastrous. An example of this appeared in 1977 in a women's magazine, which popularized the research of a Cambridge consultant suggesting that the stress induced by emancipation would increase women's testosterone levels, and produce excess hair.

11 It is not only critics of the research, like ourselves, who link the re-emergence of interest in sex differences to the development of the Women's Liberation Movement. In her introduction to *Males and Females* Hutt writes, 'The recent interest in the differences between males and females is no doubt due to the efforts of certain movements directed at social change' (Hutt 1972:17). Also at several points in the book she argues explicitly against hypotheses that she attributes to the Women's Liberation Movement or to 'feminist activists'. (See Hutt 1972:101, 138.) Again parallels may be drawn between the rise of the black civil rights movement and militant black consciousness in the USA, and the revival of interest in the relationship between race and IQ.

12 Other related areas include race and IQ (see Note 9); XYY and criminality (see e.g. Beckwith and King 1974); aggression (see e.g. Reynolds 1976); and, more generally, sociobiology (see e.g. Sahlins 1977).

13 Many detailed criticisms have been made of particular theories. For example, Singer and Montgomery (1969) and Parlee (1972) have both criticized the work of Broverman *et al.* (1968), who replied to the former criticism (Broverman *et al.* 1969). Archer (1971) commented on the work of Gray and Buffery (1971). Archer (1976 and 1978) criticizes a whole range of the biological theories that have been proposed. Marshall (1973) and Fairweather (1976) have criticized the brain lateralization theories, and DeFries *et al.* (1976) and Bouchard and McGee (1977) have both criticized the hypothesis that spatial ability is inherited via a sex-linked recessive gene.

14 For a fuller account of the production of scientific knowledge and the nature of scientific activity see: Women and Science Collective (1975); Rose and Rose (1976); any issue of *Radical Science Journal*; Griffiths, Irvine, and Miles (in press).

15 The importance of 'human nature' arguments in the ideology of women's oppression is discussed by Brunsdon (1978).

16 This in itself reflects a particular approach to the subject area. Hochschild points out that, although many psychologists are concerned with *sex differences*, sociologists most commonly consider '*sex roles* and the norms which govern them'. Alternative perspectives include concern with '*women as a minority group*' and the '*politics of caste*' (Hochschild 1973:1,013).

17 In their discussion of 'spatial ability' Buffery and Gray (1972) refer to tasks involving a wide range of measures: 'visually guided reaching and grasping behaviour in boys as young as two weeks of age'; measures of spatial ability from the Stanford-Binet intelligence test; tests of block design, picture completion, and object assembly (all subtests of the Wechsler intelligence test); tests of 'perceptual field dependence' (the rod-and-frame test and the embedded figures test);

tracking tasks (motor skills in which 'the spatial element is obviously strong'); rotary pursuit tasks (involving subjects varying in age from five to seventy years); and various tests of mechanical ability (assembling objects and toys) and mechanical reasoning since 'there is a high correlation between mechanical aptitude and spatial ability'. Referring to all these, the authors comment that 'the spatial element is clear in most of the tests we have just discussed'. They go on to consider tests subjected to factor analysis, the results of which were summarized by Guilford (1967). On these, men performed better on seven tests, six of which involve visual-spatial ability. However, one of the ten tests on which women performed better also involved this factor. Buffery and Gray account for this by suggesting 'this might well be due, as Guilford suggests (p.405) to the memory element in this test, for women tend to do better than men on memory tests in general'.

Their assumption that the nature of the ability involved in any particular task is clear, underlies their further point that 'male superiority on visual tasks only appears when manipulation of spatial relationships is involved'. It appears that women perform better on tasks such as symbol identity tests, and tests of visual matching and visual search, 'which are predictive of good performance on clerical tasks', and which 'depend for their execution principally on the discrimination and/or comparison of fine visual detail' (Buffery and Gray 1972: 125-27).

18 Comparisons of this kind are such an integral part of their theorizing that Buffery and Gray find it appropriate to comment: 'in the nature of the case it it difficult to investigate sex differences in linguistic ability in animals other than man' (Buffery and Gray 1972:130).

19 This example was pointed out by Lloyd (1976:19).

20 An example of this appears in Hutt (1972:101) where she discusses a finding that women academics published less than men of equal status, qualifications, and experience, and that this occurred irrespective of discipline and domestic commitment. Hutt suggests 'that men more often have a capacity for divergent and imaginative thinking, as well as a greater drive to bring their ideas to fruition'. This difference is presumably biologically based. What Hutt ignores is the psychological consequences and conflicts for women that result from being successful in a 'man's world'. There is a vast amount of evidence on this topic. See Note 21, Women and Science Collective (1975), and Griffiths (1978).

21 See also studies of 'fear of success' and 'locus of control' (summarized by Mednick and Weissman 1975).

22 For further discussion of this see, for example, Lehrman (1970), Rose (1976b).

23 The difficulty of attempting to blur or cross disciplinary boundaries

was clearly illustrated in the discussion following the initial presentation of this paper at the Conference. Several people challenged us because they felt that we were 'asking psychologists to be sociologists'. For further discussion of this issue see, for example, Holland (1977).

24 For further discussion of socialization theories of sex-role development see e.g. Oakley (1972), Maccoby and Jacklin (1974), Bellotti (1975), Sharpe (1976).

25 Although Lynn adopts a social learning perspective, while Chodorow's is psychoanalytic, they both argue that girls' and boys' development are not parallel. For girls, development is more continuous because their initial object of identification, their mother, remains the appropriate object. Boys have to break from their mother and learn to identify with a more remote father. Lynn has also specifically suggested that this may have consequences for sex differences in cognitive style.

26 The pamphlet does not take a clear position but states: 'There is strong evidence to support the view that there is a basic natural interest amongst girls for work involving "people", whereas boys appear more interested in "things" and their operation. How much this derives from early influences and how much from innate tendencies is discussed in the recently published researches of Corinne Hutt. . .' (ILEA 1975:13).

27 The mass media are not slow to exploit this, and many advertisements involve a more of less explicit appeal to the authority of science, whether the product being sold is toilet cleaners, skin-care products, dog food, or ethical pharmaceuticals. Television programmes on science, like *Tomorrow's World* and *Horizon* tend to reinforce rather than challenge this image.

28 Very briefly, we would argue that women's role in the family as mother and domestic worker is vital to the maintenance of the present labour force, and also to the production of the next generation. Similarly, women's role in production outside the home is to provide a cheap, and to a certain extent expendable, labour force. Both roles are vital to the maintenance of the capitalist economic system, and have important psychological consequences for women and men.

References

ALAYA, F. (1977) Victorian science and the 'genius' of woman. *Journal of the History of Ideas* **XXXVIII**:261-80.
ANDERSON, E.G. (1874) Sex in mind and education: A reply. *Fortnightly Review* **15**:582-94 (cited by Burstyn).

ARCHER, J. (1971) Sex differences in emotional behaviour: A reply to Gray and Buffery. *Acta Psychologica* **35**:415-29.

—— (1976) Biological explanations of psychological sex differences. In, B.B. Lloyd and J. Archer (eds), *Exploring Sex Differences*. London: Academic Press.

—— (1978) Biological explanations of sex role stereotypes. In, J. Chetwynd and O. Hartnett (eds), *The Sex Role System*. London: Routledge and Kegan Paul.

ARGYLE, M. and COOK, M. (1976) *Gaze and Mutual Gaze*. Cambridge: Cambridge University Press.

BAIN, A. (1875) *Mental Science*. New York: Appleton (cited by Shields).

BARKER-BENFIELD, G.J. (1976) *The Horrors of the Half-Known Life*. London: Harper and Row.

BEBEL, A. (1879) *Woman under Socialism*. New York: Schocken Books (1971).

BECKWITH, J. and KING, J. (1974) The XYY Syndrome: a dangerous myth. *New Scientist* **64**:474-76.

BELLOTTI, E.G. (1975) *Little Girls*. London: Writers and Readers Publishing Co-operative.

BERRY, J.W. (1966) Temne and Eskimo perceptual skills. *International Journal of Psychology* **1**:207-29.

BLOCK, J.H. (1976) Issues problems and pitfalls in assessing sex differences. *Merrill Palmer Quarterly* **22**:283-308.

BOUCHARD, T.J., Jr. and McGEE, M.G. (1977) Sex differences in human spatial ability: not an X-linked recessive gene effect. *Social Biology* **24**:332-35.

BOX, H. (1973) *Organisation in Animal Communities*. London: Butterworth.

BROVERMAN, D.M., KLAIBER, E.L., KOBAYASHI, Y., and VOGEL, W. (1968) Roles of activation and inhibition in sex differences in cognitive abilities. *Psychological Review* **75**:23-50.

—— (1969) Reply to the 'comment' by Singer and Montgomery on 'Roles of activation and inhibition in sex differences in cognitive abilities'. *Psychological Review* **76**:328-31.

BROWN, R. (1965) *Social Psychology*. New York: Free Press.

BRUNSDON, C. (1978) 'It is well known that by nature women are inclined to be rather personal'. In, Women's Studies Group (eds), *Women Take Issue*. London: Hutchinson.

BUFFERY, A.W.H. and GRAY, J.A. (1972) Sex differences in the development of spatial and linguistic skills. In, C. Ounsted and D.C. Taylor (eds), *Gender Differences: Their Ontogeny and Significance*. Edinburgh and London: Churchill Livingstone.

BULLOUGH, V. and VOGHT, M. (1973) Women, menstruation and nineteenth century medicine. *Bulletin of the History of Medicine*. **47**: 66-82.

BURSTYN, J.N. (1973) Education and sex: The medical case against higher education for women in England, 1870-1900. *Proceedings of the American Philosophical Society* **117**:79-89.

CENTRE FOR SCIENCE EDUCATION, CHELSEA COLLEGE (1975) *Girls and science education: cause for concern?* Nuffield Foundation, London.

CHODOROW, N. (1971) Being and doing: A cross-cultural examination of the socialization of males and females. In, V. Gornick and B.K. Moran (eds), *Woman in Sexist Society*. New York: Basic Books.

——(1974) Family structure and feminine personality. In, M.Z. Rosaldo and L. Lamphere (eds), *Woman, Culture and Society*. Stanford: Stanford University Press.

CLARKE, E.H. (1873) *Sex in Education: Or, a Fair Chance for Girls*. Boston: James R., Osgood and Co. (cited by Burstyn).

COLTHEART, M. (1975) Sex and learning differences. *New Behaviour* **1**:54-7.

COLTHEART, M., HULL, E., and SLATER, D. (1975) Sex differences in imagery and reading. *Nature* **253**:438-40.

COWARD, R. (1978) The making of the feminine – rereading Freud. *Spare Rib* **70**:43-6.

DAWSON, J.L.M. (1972) Effects of sex hormones on cognitive style in rats and men. *Behaviour Genetics* **2**:21-42.

DE FRIES, J.C., ASHTON, G.C., JOHNSON, R.C., KUSE, A.R., McCLEARN, G.E., Mi, M.P., RASHAD, M.N., VANDENBERG, S.G. and WILSON J.R. (1976) Parent-offspring resemblance for specific cognitive abilities in two ethnic groups. *Nature* **261**:131-33.

DUFFEY, E.B. (1874) *No Sex in Education*. Philadelphia (cited by Burstyn).

ELLIS, H. (1903) Variation in man and woman. *Popular Science Monthly* **62**:237-53

FAIRWEATHER, H. (1976) Sex differences in cognition. *Cognition* **4**:231-80.

FEE, E. (1976) Science and the woman problem. In, M.S. Teitelbaum (ed.), *Sex Differences*. New York: Anchor Press/Doubleday.

GARAI, J.E. and SCHEINFELD, A. (1968) Sex differences in mental and behavioural traits. *Genetic Psychology Monographs* **77**:169-299.

GEDDES, P. and THOMSON, J.A. (1889) *The Evolution of Sex* (cited by Alaya).

GRAY, J.A. and BUFFERY, A.W.H. (1971) Sex differences in emotional and cognitive behaviour in mammals including man: adaptive and neural bases. *Acta Psychologica* **35**:89-111.

GRIFFITHS, D. (1978) Hell for a woman. *Icon* **14** (or available in mimeograph from the author).

GRIFFITHS, D., IRVINE, J., and MILES, I. (in press) Social statistics: towards a radical science. In, J. Irvine, I. Miles, and J. Evans (eds), *Demystifying Social Statistics*. London: Pluto Press.

GUILFORD, J.P. (1967) *The Nature of Human Intelligence*. New York: McGraw-Hill.

HALLER, J.S. and HALLER, R.M. (1974) *The Physician and Sexuality in Vic-*

torian America. Urbana: University of Illinois Press.

HEIM, A.W. (1970) *Intelligence and Personality*. Harmondsworth: Penguin.

HOCHSCHILD, A.R. (1973) A review of sex role research. *American Journal of Sociology* 78:1011-28.

HOLLAND, R. (1977) *Self and Social Context*. London: Macmillan.

HOLLINGWORTH, L.S. (1914) Variability as related to sex differences in achievement: A critique. *American Journal of Sociology* 19:510-30.

HOWE, J.W. (1874) *Sex and education: a reply to Dr. E.H. Clarke's Sex in Education*. Boston (cited by Burstyn).

HUTT, C. (1972 *Males and Females*. Harmondsworth: Penguin.

——(1974) Sex: what's the difference? *New Scientist* 62:405-7.

ILEA (1975) *Careers Opportunities for Girls*. London: ILEA.

KAMIN, L. (1974) *The Science and Politics of IQ*. New York: Lawrence Erbaum.

KELLY, A. (1974) *An unfair profession: A review of the position of British Women in Science*. Edinburgh University Centre for Educational Sociology (unpublished).

LEHRAM, D.S. (1970) Semantic and conceptual issues in the nature-nurture problem. In, L.R. Aronson, E. Tobach, D.S. Lehram, and J.S. Rosenblatt (eds), *The Development and Evolution of Behavior*. San Fransisco: Freeman.

LLOYDS, B.B. (1976) Social responsibility and research on sex differences. In, B.B. Lloyd and J. Archer (eds), *Exploring Sex Differences*. London: Academic Press.

LLOYD, B.B. and ARCHER, J. (eds) (1976) *Exploring Sex Differences*. London: Academic Press.

LYNN, D.B. (1962) Sex role and parental identification. *Child Development* 33:555-64.

MacARTHUR, R. (1967) Sex differences in field dependence for the Eskimo. *International Journal of Psychology* 2:139-40.

McCLAREN, L. (1888-90) The fallacy of the superiority of man. *The Woman's World* 1:59 (cited by Alaya).

MACCOBY, E.E. and JACKLIN, C.N. (1974) *The Psychology of Sex Differences*. Stanford, Calif.: Stanford University Press.

MARSHALL, J. (1973) Some problems associated with recent accounts of hemispheric specialization. *Neuropsychologia* 11:463-69.

MARX, K. (1954) *Capital* (vol. I.) London: Lawrence and Wishart.

MAUDSLEY, H. (1874) Sex in mind and in education. *Fortnightly Review* 15: 466-83 (cited by Burstyn).

MEDNICK, M.T.S. and WEISSMAN, H.J. (1975) The psychology of women – selected topics. *Annual Review of Psychology* 26:1-18.

43

MILL, J.S. (1869) *The Subjection of Women*. London: Dent (1965).

MITCHELL, J. (1974) *Psychoanalysis and Feminism*. London: Allen Lane.

MONEY, J., HAMPSON, J.G., and HAMPSON, J.L. (1955) Hermaphroditism: recommendations concerning assignment of sex, change of sex and psychologic measurement. *Bulletin Johns Hopkins Hospital* **97**:284-300.

——(1957) Imprinting and the establishment of gender role. *Archives of Neurology and Psychiatry* **77**:333-36.

MOORE, W.W. (1886) President at the 54th Annual Meeting of the British Medical Association as reported in the *Lancet* **2**:315.

OAKLEY, A. (1972) *Sex, Gender and Society*. London: Temple Smith.

——(1974) *Housewife*. London: Allen Lane.

O'FAOLAIN, V. and MARTINES, L. (1973) *Not in God's Image*. London: Temple Smith.

PARLEE, M.B. (1972) Comments on 'Roles of activation and inhibition in sex differences in cognitive abilities' by D.M. Broverman, E.L. Klaiber, Y. Kobayashi and W. Vogel, *Psychological Review* **79**:180-84.

PATRICK, G.T.W. (1895) The Psychology of women. *Popular Science Monthly* **47**:209-25.

PFEIFFER, E. (1888) *Woman and Work*. London (cited by Burstyn).

REYNOLDS, V. (1976) *The Biology of Human Action*. San Fransisco: Freeman.

RICHARDSON, K., SPEARS, D., and RICHARDS, M. (eds) (1972) *Race, Culture and Intelligence*. Harmondsworth: Penguin.

ROMANES, G.J. (1887) Mental differences between the sexes. *Nineteenth Century* **21**:654-72.

ROSE, S. (1976a) *The Conscious Brain*. Harmondsworth: Penguin.

——(1976b) Scientific racism and ideology: the IQ racket from Galton to Jensen. In, H. Rose and S. Rose (eds), *The Political Economy of Science*. London: Macmillan.

ROSE, H. and ROSE, S. (eds) (1976) *The Political Economy of Science*. London: Macmillan.

ROSENBERG, C.S. and ROSENBERG, C.E. (1973) The female animal: medical and biological views of woman and her role in nineteenth century America. *Journal of American History* **LX**:332-56.

RUDINGER (1877) Cited by Shields (1975).

RUTTER, M. (1972) *Maternal Deprivation Reassessed*. Harmondsworth: Penguin.

SAHLINS, M. (1977) *The Use and Abuse of Biology*. London: Tavistock.

SCHAFFER, R. (1977) *Mothering*. London: Open Books.

SEWARD, G.H. (1944) Psychological effects of the menstrual cycle on women workers. *Psychological Bulletin* **41**:90-102.

SHARPE, S. (1976) *Just Like A Girl: How Girls Learn to be Women*. Harmondsworth: Penguin.

SHIELDS, S.A. (1975) Functionalism, Darwinism and the psychology of women: A study in social myth. *American Psychologist* **30**:739-54.

SINGER, G. and MONTGOMERY, R.B. (1969) Comment on 'Roles of activation and inhibition in sex differences in cognitive abilities'. *Psychological Review* **76**:325-27.

SLATER, P.J.B. (1977) Sociobiology and ethics. *Bulletin of the British Psychological Society* **30**:349-51.

STAFFORD, R.E. (1961) Sex differences in spatial visualisation as evidence of sex linked inheritance. *Perceptual and Motor Skills* **13**:428.

THORNDIKE, E.L. (1906) Sex in Education. *The Bookman* **23**:211-214.

——(1910) *Educational Psychology*. New York: Teachers College, Columbia University.

TIGER, L. (1969) *Men in Groups*. London: Nelson.

TORRANCE, E.P. (1963) Changing reactions of pre-adolescent girls to tasks requiring creative scientic thinking. *Journal of Genetic Psychology* **102**:217-23.

WALKER, A. (1850) *Woman Physiologically Considered*. New York: Langley (cited by Shields).

WITELSON, S.F. (1976) Sex and the single hemisphere: specialization of the right hemisphere for spatial processing. *Science* **193**:425-27.

WOMEN AND SCIENCE COLLECTIVE (1975) *Science for People*. Special Issue **29**.

WOOD, A.D. (1973) 'The fashionable diseases': Women's complaints and their treatment in nineteenth-century America. *Journal of Interdisciplinary History* **IV**:25-52.

WOOLLEY, H.T. (1910) Psychological Literature; A review of the recent literature on the psychology of sex. *Psychological Bulletin* **7**:335-42.

TWO

On the description of psychological sex differences

JANET SAYERS

Psychologists have produced evidence to support the description of individuals as masculine or feminine, and the characterization of women as maternal, dependent, social, suggestible, and submissive. In this paper I shall consider the validity of these descriptions of the data, and the expectations that have influenced them.

Sex differences as evidence of masculinity/femininity

One way in which psychologists have described sex differences has been in terms of masculinity-femininity. Thus, for example, the different toy choices of boys and girls have been described as 'masculine' and 'feminine' respectively (e.g. Fagot and Patterson 1969),[1] and children who make predominantly masculine toy choices have been described as 'preferring the masculine role', whilst those making predominantly feminine toy choices have

46

been characterized as 'preferring the feminine role' (Brown 1957). Sex differences in questionnaire responses have also been used as a measure of masculinity-femininity (e.g. Terman and Miles 1936). In this case an item response is described as 'masculine' if it accords with the male norm, 'feminine' if it accords with the female norm (as established in the standardization of the test). An individual's masculinity or femininity is then computed by adding together his/her masculine responses and, where necessary, subtracting his/her feminine responses.

The validity of using toy choices or questionnaire responses to determine an individual's masculinity-femininity rests on the assumption that these responses may legitimately be described as 'masculine' or 'feminine' simply on the basis that they are made more often by one sex than by the other. That is, it assumes that any behavioural sex difference is relevant to masculinity-femininity. Psychologists themselves disagree, however, as to whether this is a valid procedure.

Maccoby and Jacklin imply that this procedure may correspond to common parlance at least where sex differences in toy choices are concerned. They say that: '. . . it is possible that societies begin to label as "masculine" those toys that differentially attract boys even if there is no relationship of the toy to a masculine role' (Maccoby and Jacklin 1975:278). Kohlberg disputes the description of toy preferences as indicative of masculinity or femininity. He claims that: 'These early sex differences are specific interest differences; they are not a reflection of general masculinity-femininity values. . .' (Kohlberg 1966:112). Constantinople, in her review of masculinity-femininity scales, also disputes the view that any questionnaire response that discriminates reliably between the sexes can, on that basis alone, be scored as masculine or feminine. She says of masculinity-femininity tests that:

'In some cases, item content would appear to be logically related to an intuitive definition of masculinity or femininity, but in many other cases the content seems to be irrelevant to any identifiable definition of the concept.' (Constantinople 1973:390)[2]

The indiscriminate description of sex differences as indicative of masculinity-femininity thus remains controversial. That the sexes differ on a particular behavioural measure cannot, therefore, on its own be an adequate reason for describing that measure as masculine or feminine. Until more agreed criteria are used to judge the construct validity of particular test items the acccuracy of describing an individual as masculine or feminine on the basis of his or her responses to those items cannot properly be assessed.

Women as essentially maternal

If some psychologists have equated behavioural sex differences with masculinity-femininity, others have assimilated them to the sexual division of labour in reproduction. Gray and Buffery maintain, for instance, that:

> 'sex differences in emotional and cognitive behaviour among mammalian species [including man]. . . are all remote but necessary consequences of the same overriding fact: the division of labour between the sexes in reproductive behaviour.' (Gray and Buffery 1971:106-7)

In particular, they argue, as does Hutt, that the psychological characteristics of women fit them for the reproductive task of child-rearing. Hutt, for example, lists the female skills of 'nurture and repair' (Hutt 1972:107), 'the greater conformity and consistency of the female', and women's 'greater emphasis and reliance on linguistic skills and moral propensities' (1972:133) as adapted to this task. And she concludes, in general, that: 'A woman's primary role is that of motherhood and most women have some or other of the attributes which fit them for this role' (Hutt 1972:136).

Let us consider first the cognitive behaviours that are supposed to fit women for motherhood. Gray and Buffery admit that the connection of female superiority in verbal skills with the female role in reproduction is 'remote'. They claim, nevertheless, that the linguistic skill of women is essentially related to child-rearing, to the task of teaching infants to speak. Other psychologists are not so catholic in the sex differences they include as relevant to adult reproductive roles. Maccoby and Jacklin, for instance, say that: 'It is difficult to determine what behaviors are, and what are not, linked to sex roles. The mere existence of a behavioral sex difference does not constitute evidence of such

48

linkage' (Maccoby and Jacklin 1975:277). And they specifically imply that sex differences in perceptual and cognitive skills are irrelevant to the different roles of the two sexes.

When we look at the personality traits that are supposed to distinguish women from men, we find similar uncertainty about the relevance of these traits to child-rearing. Bardwick, for instance, is quite unclear as to whether the feminine trait of passivity is relevant to this task. She sometimes argues that it is relevant, that it is 'a preferred coping technique at particular times such as during pregnancy or in those years when one is nurturing very young children' (Bardwick 1971:125), whilst elsewhere she claims that passivity is irrelevant to maternity, that 'motherhood, which is the essence of femininity, is active and not passive' (1971:7).

Nilsson's (1970) research on the adaptation of 'masculine' and 'feminine' women to pregnancy reflects a similar inconsistency regarding the relevance of feminine traits to maternity. He found that women who assessed themselves as more feminine (e.g. gentle, emotional, dependent) reported more psychiatric symptoms during pregnancy than those who assessed themselves as more masculine (e.g. strong, self-confident). This finding certainly suggests that some so-called 'feminine' traits are not only not relevant but are maladapted to maternity. Nilsson, however, drew the opposite conclusion. He suggested that the 'masculine' women wished to appear 'healthy', and, for this reason, denied their psychiatric symptoms. They were, therefore, by implication at least, less well adapted to maternity than the 'feminine' women. In sum, Nilsson implies that feminine traits fit women better for maternity than do masculine traits although his data suggest the opposite conclusion.

Despite the apparent inconsistency between Nilsson's data and his conclusion, his research is to be welcomed if only because it relates data on psychological femininity to data on maternal adjustment. For, despite the plethora of claims of a fit between femininity and maternity,[3] there has been all too little empirical research into the evidence for such a close link. There is also an urgent need for data regarding the psychological traits (which might equally characterize men and women) that are actually associated with successful child-rearing in this society.

The decision as to what constitutes 'successful child-rearing'

obviously involves moral questions. But, in the absence of adequate research into this issue, pronouncements as to which traits
should be described as relevant to this task will remain purely
ideological. This is reflected in the statements of the psychologists, cited above, regarding the relevance of particular traits to
child-rearing. Such pronouncements appear to reflect these
psychologists' personal views about the proper social role of
women, rather than any relevant findings about the psychology
of child-rearing. Thus, Hutt's apparent willingness to describe
virtually all female psychological traits by reference to their
child-rearing function appears to stem from her view that
motherhood is, and should be, 'woman's primary role' (Hutt
1972:136). Bardwick (1971), who is more uncertain than Hutt
about the proper social role of women, accordingly feels more
uneasy about describing all feminine behaviour in terms of the
single social role of maternity. Lastly, Maccoby and Jacklin's
(1975) refusal to regard psychological sex differences as coter-
minous with the division of labour between the sexes is consistent with their view that this division of labour is not sacrosanct.

Women as dependent, social, suggestible, and submissive

If psychologists have failed to determine adequately the validity
of describing particular female traits as relevant or irrelevant to
their maternal role, they have provided much more evidence to
substantiate the description of girls and women as more dependent, social, submissive, and suggestible than boys and men.
Thus, for instance, Goldberg and Lewis's (1967) findings concerning sex difference in the play behaviour of one-year-olds were
interpreted by them as corroborating the expectation that girls
are more dependent than boys. They base this conclusion on the
observation that one-year-old girls stayed closer to their mothers
in an observation room than did boys of the same age. When
dependency is measured by the degree to which the toddler cries
when the mother leaves the room then boys sometimes appear to
be more dependent than girls (e.g. Feldman and Ingham 1973).
Having compared the results of using different measures of
dependency Maccoby and Jacklin (1975) conclude that the
description of girls as more dependent than boys is not warranted
by the data.

   These authors cite many other instances in the research on sex differences where psychologists have used one or two measures of a sex-typed trait – such as sociability, suggestibility, or submissiveness – and have described their findings in terms of this trait. They argue that, in many cases, this involves an unwarranted extrapolation from the data. When other measures of the trait are used no sex difference, or a sex difference opposite from that predicted on the basis of sex-role stereotypes, is often found. In sum, Maccoby and Jacklin imply that psychologists would be well advised to describe observed sex differences in terms of the actual measures used rather than in terms of expectations based on sex-role stereotypes.

Research into sex–role stereotypes

Since expectations about psychological sex differences have so bedevilled the description of observed behaviour, it is appropriate that psychologists should have sought to determine what our actual expectations are in this matter. An influential study in this respect is that by Rosenkrantz *et al.* (1968). These researchers asked college students to list the behaviours, attitudes, and personality characteristics that they considered to differentiate men and women. The items generated in this way were then arranged in bipolar form, one pole being characterized as typically masculine, the other as typically feminine. The forty-one items on which there was 75 per cent or better agreement between students (as to which pole characterized men and which women) were designated 'stereotypic items'.

These stereotypic items parallel, in large measure, the expectations that seem to have guided psychologists in their description of observed sex differences in behaviour. The students in Rosenkrantz's sample expected men to be more aggressive, self-confident, ambitious, and objective than women, and more able than women to separate feelings from ideas. On the other hand, they expected women to be more easily influenced, dependent, excitable, emotional, talkative, and interested in their own appearance than men. Psychologists have described the differences between the sexes in very similar terms. They have characterized men as more aggressive and self-confident than women; and women as more dependent, and more verbally fluent than men. They have also described women as less objective than men. Freud, for instance, said of women that they are 'more often influenced in their judgements by feelings of affection or hostility' (Freud 1925:197). Where Rosenkrantz's college students expect women to be more interested in their own appearance than men, psychoanalysts have spoken of women as the vainer sex (Mitchell 1974). And, just as these students described women as more excitable than men, so Broverman (Broverman *et al.* 1968), one of Rosenkrantz's co-workers, described women as less able to inhibit initial response than men.

The sex-role expectations tapped by Rosenkrantz's Stereotype Questionnaire may well reflect many of the expectations that psychologists hold about sex differences in behaviour. They may not, however, reflect all the sex-role expectations that have a significant effect on relations between the sexes, or on behaviour generally.

First, the questionnaire discovers only those expectations about behavioural sex differences that are conscious and easily articulated. Kohlberg points this out with reference to masculinity-femininity tests when he says that these tests 'need not represent all the important behavioural sex differences to be found in a culture. In the main, these tests reflect conscious sex-typed interests and values that are easily verbalized' (Kohlberg 1966:110). His point applies equally to the Stereotype Questionnaire.

The findings of psychoanalysis, and of anthropology, suggest that people do, indeed, hold important sex-role attitudes which, even though they may be neither conscious nor easily verbalized, nevertheless exercise a powerful effect on behaviour. Psychoanalysts, for instance, report that many of their patients view women as destructive and that this significantly affects their sexual relationships (e.g. Klein 1931). And anthropologists have also reported that, in many societies, women are regarded as dangerous because of their power to pollute men, and that this attitude significantly affects interactions between the sexes not only in some primitive societies (e.g. Douglas 1966) but also amongst gypsies in our own society (Okely 1975). It would be surprising if similar attitudes towards women were not held at some level by American college students. They are, however, unlikely to be revealed by the kind of procedure used by Rosenkrantz to assess sex-role stereotypes.

Second, just as research into the psychology of men and women has focussed on *differences* in the behaviour of the sexes (Archer

1976), so Rosenkrantz's questionnaire studies characteristics that are expected to *differentiate* the sexes.[4] This legitimates Rosenkrantz's procedure of arranging each characteristic in bipolar form with one pole as feminine, the other as masculine. This procedure, however, makes the Stereotype Questionnaire entirely insensitive to contradictions in sex-role expectations. The arrangement of the traits of submissiveness and dominance, for instance, at opposite ends of the same questionnaire item precludes the possibility of registering the expectation that women are both submissive and dominant. Yet, it is clear, simply on the basis of anecdotal observation, that woman is often regarded in this self-same contradictory fashion as, for instance, both 'living-doll' (Rowbotham 1973) and 'fishwife'.

Psychoanalytic and anthropological findings bear out this impression that people hold contradictory and inconsistent expectations of female behaviour. Psychoanalysts report many cases in which patients simultaneously expect women to be good and bad (e.g. Klein 1945), sacred and profane, virgin and whore. Philosophers have also spoken of this inconsistency in attitudes towards women. Weininger, the German philosopher, claimed, according to Klein, that there are 'two ideal types of woman . . . the Mother and the Courtesan . . . and any woman may represent both, either at the same time or at different times' (Klein 1946:61). Anthropologists have described similar contradictions in the sex-role stereotypes of non-industrial societies; Douglas (1966) shows how both sacred and polluting aspects are often attributed to women; Campbell (1964) states that the Greek shepherd community, the Sarakatsani, view women as inherently lascivious, and also expect them to be sexually modest; and Strathern claims that the Hagen of New Guinea regard women 'as at the same time soft-brained and hard-headed' (Strathern 1976:52-3). The bipolar organization of items in the Rosenkrantz Stereotype Questionnaire precludes its revealing similar contradictory expectations about female behaviour in this society.

Lastly, the neglect of unconscious and unverbalized sex-role attitudes, and of inconsistencies in these attitudes, has led to the neglect of the more powerful, albeit negative, images of women as, for instance, destructive, dangerous, and hard-headed. The feminine pole of the items included in the Rosenkrantz Questionnaire, instead, reiterates images of women as the weaker sex, as 'submissive', 'quiet', 'gentle', and as having a 'strong need for security'. This bias in the Stereotype Questionnaire again reflects a similar bias in the expectations that have guided research into psychological sex differences.

In general the psychological description of sex differences, and of sex-role stereotypes, has implied that women are, and are expected to be, uniformly the weaker sex. However, as I have indicated, this implication may well be unjustified.

Conclusion

In this paper I have sought to demonstrate that the description, by some psychologists, of psychological sex differences in terms of 'masculinity–femininity', in terms of sex roles in reproduction, or in terms of sex-typed traits (e.g. dependency), is controversial and often unwarranted; and that current research into the content of sex-role stereotypes tends to be impervious to many of the important and contradictory features of people's ideas about the differences between the sexes. Since these ideas serve an ideological function in a sexist society, in that they are often used to justify and explain existing inequalities in the social lot of men and women, research into them can have the effect of bolstering sexist ideology. Where psychologists have simply assimilated their data to sex-role stereotypes, assumed the validity and coherence of these stereotypes, and reiterated (rather than examined) the ideological assumption that sex-typed traits match the requirements of sex-typed social roles, they have tended to reinforce sexist ideology. It is to be hoped that the lead given by Maccoby and Jacklin (1975) in systematically examining the validity of sex-role stereotypes will be followed by other psychologists, and that psychology will also seek to investigate, more rigorously than it has to date, the content of these stereotypes. Only when it does this can psychology contribute to our knowledge, as opposed to our prejudices, about the psychology of men and women.

Notes

1   These researchers found, for instance, that boys preferred playing with building blocks, toy trucks, and tricycles, whilst girls preferred painting, cutting-out, doll play, and looking at books.
2   The following items included in the Terman and Miles (1936)

54

Masculinity-Femininity Test (Form A, Exercise 7) would seem to be irrelevant in this sense: 'Are you much embarrassed when you make a grammatical mistake?' 'Do people nearly always treat you right?' 'Do you hear easily when spoken to?' (An affirmative response to these items is scored feminine, a negative response masculine).

3 Rheingold (1964), for instance, goes so far as to assert that the birth of a baby is a 'degree in femininity'!

4 It might be objected that this procedure is legitimate given Rosenkrantz *et al.*'s (1968) original aim, which was to study the *differential* evaluation of traits expected of men and women. However, Rosenkrantz does not restrict himself to this aim. He draws very general conclusions about sex-role stereotypes from his results. His research has, moreover, had an influence on the literature on sex-role stereotyping that goes well beyond the findings regarding the evaluative content of these stereotypes. The Stereotype Questionnaire has been presumed, both by Rosenkrantz and by many other writers in this area, to be a true indicator of the content of sex-role stereotypes. It is the validity of this presumption that I wish to question.

References

ARCHER, J. (1976) Biological explanations of psychological sex differences. In, B. Lloyd and J. Archer (eds), *Exploring Sex Differences*. London: Academic Press.

BARDWICK, J.M. (1971) *Psychology of Women*. New York: Harper and Row.

BREEN, D. (1975) *The Birth of a First Child*. London: Tavistock.

BROVERMAN, D.K., KLAIBER, E.L., KOBAYASHI, Y., and VOGEL, W. (1968) Roles of activation and inhibition in sex differences in cognitive abilities. *Psychological Review* 75:23-50.

BROWN, D.G. (1957) Masculinity-femininity development in children. *Journal of Consulting Psychology* 21:197-202.

CAMPBELL, J. (1964) *Honour, Family and Patronage*. London: Oxford University Press.

CONSTANTINOPLE, A. (1973) Masculinity-femininity: an exception to a famous dictum? *Psychological Bulletin* 80:389-407.

DOUGLAS, M. (1966) *Purity and Danger*. London: Routledge and Kegan Paul.

FAGOT, B.I. and PATTERSON, G.R. (1969) An *in vivo* analysis of reinforcing contingencies for sex-role behaviors in the pre-school child. *Developmental Psychology* 1:563-68.

FELDMAN, S.S. and INGHAM, M.E. (1973) *Attachment behaviour: a study of the concurrent validity in two age groups*. Stanford University, unpublished manuscript, cited in Maccoby and Jacklin (1975).

FREUD, S. (1925) Some psychological consequences of the anatomical distinction between the sexes. *Collected Papers* (vol. V). London: Hogarth.

GOLDBERG, S. and LEWIS, M. (1967) Play behavior in the year-old infant: early sex differences. In, J.M. Bardwick (ed.), *Readings on the Psychology of Women*. New York: Harper and Row.

GRAY, J.A. and BUFFERY, A.W.H. (1971) Sex differences in emotional and cognitive behaviour including man: adaptive and neural bases. *Acta Psychologica* 35:89-111.

HUTT, C. (1972) *Males and Females*. Harmondsworth: Penguin.

KLEIN, MELANIE (1931) A contribution to the theory of intellectual inhibition. In, Klein (1948).

——(1945) The Oedipus Complex in the light of early anxieties. In, Klein (1948).

——(1948) *Contributions to Psycho-analysis: 1921-1945*. London: Hogarth.

KLEIN, VIOLET (1946) *The Feminine Character: History of an Ideology*. New York: International University Press, 1949.

KOHLBERG, L. (1966) A cognitive-developmental analysis of children's sex-role concepts and attitudes. In, E.E. Maccoby (ed.), *The Development of Sex Differences*. Stanford, Calif.: Stanford University Press.

MACCOBY, E.E. and JACKLIN, C.N. (1975) *The Psychology of Sex Differences*. London: Oxford University Press.

MITCHELL, J. (1974) *Psychoanalysis and Feminism*. London: Allen Lane.

NILSSON, A. (1970) Para-natal emotional adjustment: A prospective investigation of 165 women. *Acta Psychiatrica Scandinavica Supplement* 220 (cited in Breen (1975)).

OKELY, J. (1975) Gypsy women: models in conflict. In, S. Ardener (ed.), *Perceiving Women*. London: Malaby Press.

RHEINGOLD, J. (1964) *The Fear of Being a Woman*. New York: Grune and Stratton (cited in Breen (1975)).

ROSENKRANTZ, P., VOGEL, S., BEE, H., BROVERMAN, I., and BROVERMAN, D. (1968) Sex-role stereotypes and self-concepts in college students. *Journal of Consulting and Clinical Psychology* 32, 287-95.

ROWBOTHAM, S. (1973) *Woman's Consciousness, Man's World*. Harmondsworth: Penguin.

STRATHERN, M. (1976) An anthropological perspective. In, B. Lloyd and J. Archer (eds), *Exploring Sex Differences*. London: Academic Press.

TERMAN, L. and MILES, C.C. (1936) *Sex and Personality*. New York: McGraw-Hill.

WEININGER, O. (1903) *Sex and Character*. London: Heinemann, 1906 (cited in Klein (1946)).

THREE

Psychic celibacy in men

JOHN ROWAN

I am a man.

The Women's Movement has taught me that this is a contentious, problematic, and deeply social statement, not a simple truth about biology. It arouses difficulties, objections, and high feelings. It is not neutral.

I am a researcher. This, too, is a contentious statement. Most research cuts the researcher off from those studied, and makes those studied feel alienated, misjudged, and 'done to'. Nick Heather has written about this (1976) and so have I (1973;1974).

When I came to choose a Ph.D. research project, I wanted to get hold of one that would do justice to both of these problematic areas. It seemed to me that anything less would be an avoidance of what really mattered to me. But it was asking for trouble. I met every kind of obstacle, both within myself and in the outside world. So instead of this article being about the research, it is about the ideas that are going into the research. It is all starting a year late.

The research problem arises out of my own experience of being a man in relationships with women. One of the things I have found to operate as a barrier in such relations is a real distaste for certain ways of thinking, feeling, and acting which I find in women. I don't like being submissive; I don't like serving others; I don't like feelings being too near the surface, or being at the mercy of my feelings; I don't like gossip about neighbours or talk about relatives; I don't like being too patient . . . there is a long list of these things. And they all have one thing in common – these are all things that remind me of my mother and not of my father. It is as if I had at some time made a note of all the things that remind me of my mother and given myself an instruction: 'Don't be like that.'

Then in 1976 I heard Margaret Mead talking at the APA Conference in Washington, and she was saying that the main difference between boys and girls in our patriarchal culture is that they both have a mother; but while the girl is taught to be like her and emulate her, the boy is taught to be unlike her – he is taught that this is the way not to be; it is an inferior way to be.

So it seemed that my problem – a problem that made it hard for me to relate to women because basically I saw all these ways of thinking, feeling, and acting as inferior – might be wider than being just a private difficulty of mine. But, still, that is where the initial impetus came from, and where it still comes from, because I have found that being aware of this prejudice as a prejudice is not enough to dispel it. I still suffer from it.

Over the past five years or so I have read a great deal of the literature of the Men's Movement that was stimulated by feminism. It has much to say about the oppressiveness of men's work roles, and the equal oppressiveness of the way in which feelings have become relatively inaccessible to men.

But one of the difficulties in this field has been the lack of any very good empirical theories or even concepts. The concept of a role is itself open to a good deal of criticism, and the concept of a sex role pushes an already tricky idea to its very limit. Even if it were to be made more robust, this concept still is not integrated into any wider framework.

I was therefore very excited when I came across the notion of psychic celibacy. As stated by Bianchi it seemed to me to be neat, narrow, specific, and testable. He says:

'. . . placing women in heaven (Mary) or hell (Eve) became a convenient way of removing her from earth where she would compete with men for a just share of material and human resources . . . I have labelled this well-entrenched masculine mentality as psychic celibacy. Although distinct from physical celibacy as practised in Catholicism, psychic celibacy is a more pervasive and imposing phenomenon. It consists in keeping women mentally and emotionally at arms' length. It is in fact the core dogma of our patriarchal era. Women can be exalted as wife, virgin, mother or deprecated (and enjoyed) as temptress, playmate, whore. In whatever way this male projection works, woman is object, non-equal, manipulated, distanced . . . Such a world is profoundly celibate . . .' (Bianchi and Reuther 1976)

The field at present

It would be good, at this point, to set psychic celibacy in a research context, so that it could be seen what other people had said on the subject. But there is no research on psychic celibacy existing at present (or at least none known to me). There are, however, three main areas of work that do bear on the question and have some relevance to it.

ROLE THEORY

The first of these is role theory, which includes a good deal of writing on sex roles. It draws on the anthropological evidence of people like Margaret Mead (1950), Barry *et al.* (1957), Murdock (1937), and others, which seem to show, as D'Andrade (1970) points out, that the ways in which men and women are expected to behave are influenced by 'which sex controls economic capital, the extent and kind of division of labour by sex, the degree of political "authoritarianism" and family composition'.

There is of course a great deal of work now on sex-role socialization, and it all seems to show that it is a very *heavy* process, with a lot of concentrated weight behind it to make it happen. It is no good saying what is obviously true, as Duberman (1975) does: 'To be born with a penis does not ensure that one will be brave . . . Having ovaries does not assure a girl that she will love housework'. Kagan (1964) wrote a good summary of the work done up to that point, demonstrating this point quite adequately.

The research shows that a whole set of qualities are expected of boys and men. As Broverman *et al.* (1970) have demonstrated, they include such things as:

aggressive	not easily influenced
dominant	acts as a leader
competitive	self-confident

These are all masculine qualities.

However the independent work of Bem (1974) found the masculine qualities to include:

aggressive	acts like a leader
dominant	willing to take a stand
competitive	strong personality

It seems clear that the stereotype is very well fixed and well known. It is not, however, always easy to live up to. Sidney Jourard (1971) wrote a paper, quoting a good deal of research, on 'Some lethal aspects of the male role', in which he showed that the effort to live up to it can easily result in poor mental health and even the shortening of life. Studies by Maccoby (1966) have shown that boys who identify strongly with their own sex roles tend to be less intelligent and creative than those who identify less rigidly with members of their own sex. And Harford *et al.* (1967) found that sex-typed identification among adult males is associated with low self-acceptance, high anxiety, and neuroticism.

And all this starts very early. Ruth Hartley reported research showing that:

'boys are aware of what is expected of them because they are boys and restrict their interests and activities to what is suitably "masculine" in the kindergarten, while girls amble gradually in the direction of "feminine" patterns for five more years. In other words, more stringent demands are made on boys than on girls, and at an early age, when they are least able to understand either the reasons for or the nature of the demands.' (Hartley 1959)

She continues with some remarks that are of direct relevance to our present concerns:

'. . . a great many boys do give evidence of anxiety centred in the whole area of sex-connected role behaviours, an anxiety which frequently expresses itself in over-straining to be masculine, in virtual panic at being caught doing anything traditionally defined as feminine, and in hostility toward anything even hinting at "femininity", including females themselves.'

(Hartley 1959)

It is precisely this kind of panic that is most effective in producing neurotic defences of one kind and another, and moreover those that are most enduring and hard to change.

The difficulties are again made worse by the fact that in the vast majority of families, the father is not at home nearly as much as the mother. Often the boy never actually sees the father doing his real daily-life activities at all. So the information he gets about proper masculine behaviour is limited and distorted. There is plenty of information on television, but it is hard to distinguish between fact and fiction, and media images are in any case highly selected in the direction of reinforcing existing stereotypes, in the vast majority of cases. The main source of information for boys is, therefore, the peer group of other boys. But since they have no better sources of information than he has, all they can do is to pool the impressions and anxieties they derived from their early training. Ruth Hartley ends her paper by saying:

'When he sees women as weak, easily damaged, lacking strength in mind and in body, able to perform only the tasks which require the least strength and are of least importance, what boy in his right senses would not give his all to escape this alternative to the male role? For many, unfortunately, the scramble to escape takes on all the aspects of panic, and the outward semblance of non-femininity is achieved at a tremendous cost of anxiety and self-alienation. From our data, we would infer that the degree of anxiety experienced has a direct relationship to the degree of pressure to be "manly" exerted on the boy, the rigidity of the pattern to which he is pressed to conform, the availability of a good model, and the apparent degree of success which his efforts achieve.'

(Hartley 1959)

The results of this process are easy to pick up. As Sexton (1969) has said, the research shows that children have already picked up their dislike for the women's role by the age of four. By kindergarten about half the girls prefer the father's role and about a quarter of the boys prefer the mother's role. By twelve or thirteen, girls who act like boys are much more socially accepted than boys who act like girls. Among adults, 20 to 31 per cent of women prefer the male social role, while only 2 to 4 per cent of men prefer the women's role.

Enough has been said to indicate that role theory has quite a lot to contribute in the way of background material for our study. From the point of view of role theory, psychic celibacy would be a necessary mechanism for the maintenance of sex-role differences. It might well be functional for a society based on the division of labour by sex, even though, as we have seen, it is clearly dysfunctional for the mental health of many people, both men and women. For the criticism of the division of labour along sex or gender lines, we have to turn to the second of the three main areas of work that are relevant.

PATRIARCHY THEORY

Patriarchy theory is much more recent, and there is much less material available, particularly material relevant to the position of men.

One of the clearest writers on the subject is Sheila Jeffreys (see e.g. Jeffreys and Hodson 1977). She draws convincing parallels between the class struggle and the sex struggle, the one being based on the mode of production and the other on the mode of reproduction. Just as in the one case the struggle is for the working class to take over and run the mode of production differently, so in the other the struggle is for women to take over and run the mode of reproduction differently. On this sort of view, the question of sex roles becomes highly political. The kinds of masculine values and attributes that we saw in the previous section now become the essential buttresses of a hostile system that needs to be dismantled.

In particular, the quality of aggression, which we saw in the previous section, becomes not just a neutral quality, valuable in some circumstances and disadvantageous in others – it becomes an important key to the whole system. Patriarchy is seen as essentially depending on violence for its continuance and women are forced into feeling fearful, inferior, and inadequate so that they do not even contemplate revolt. Women like Atkinson (1974) have even put forward the view that men generally hate women in a quite direct and personal way. And this view receives support from people like the psychoanalyst Robert Seidenberg who says:

'Although it is a vast oversimplification to attribute mental illness to one cause, we are becoming aware of social forces that filter down to the family and mother-child unit. The effects of a male-dominated society on "mothering" cannot be overlooked as potentially and actually disintegrative . . . In the unconscious of men as found in psychoanalysis, there is a deep-seated fear and loathing of women. All the songs of love do not displace this underlying contempt for those "unfortunates" with gaping wounds where a penis ought to be. It is the loathing of differences that encourages and maintains the male homosexual cultures from which females are regularly excluded.'   (Seidenberg 1973)

The difference between an enlightened Freudian like this and a humanistic psychologist is that we do not see any of this as inevitable. It is because the 'fear and loathing' is permitted and encouraged by a million social forms that it becomes powerful. If it were denied by the culture, it would become an individual quirk with few consequences.

But at least this makes it clear that when feminists are accused of man-hating they are quite right to suggest that the general culture of society is women-hating, and that this is the major problem.

Not that it is only women who are seeing the breakdown of patriarchy as a key political issue. Men, too, have seen the need for change as something that affects them in positive ways. Books like those of Farrell (1975), Goodman and Walby (1975), Korda (1975), and Nichols (1975) all see that the change is one which is badly needed if men are to be whole persons, and not fragmented and one-sided apologies for human beings.

From this point of view, then, the major movement of our time is the breakdown of patriarchy, and it therefore makes a lot of sense to find out exactly how patriarchy works, and how it changes. From this point of view, psychic celibacy is an important bastion of the patriarchal system. With the breakdown of this system, it becomes a dysfunctional survival. How can it be changed? Any answers that can be obtained to this can contribute towards a new and more detailed theory of patriarchy and its breakdown.

CONSCIOUSNESS THEORY

The third body of theory to which psychic celibacy seems to be relevant is more speculative and even more new.

Robert Ornstein (1972) has brought together a great deal of work, all of which seems to suggest that all human beings have access to the two major forms of mental functioning. One is a 'right-handed' form, which is rational, active, linear, and masculine; the other is a 'left-handed' form, which is intuitive, receptive, non-linear, and feminine. Our culture, he says, has approved and encouraged the right-hand form, and ignored or denigrated the left-hand form.

So we here have a split within the person instead of, as previously, the split or opposition between people. Each person in our culture is encouraged to play up and respect the right-handed approach, and to play down and disrespect the left-handed one. Thus there is a kind of internal oppression, such that when people use intuition or indulge in non-linear thinking they feel guilty, as if they were not doing it in the proper way – the 'right' way.

Stan Gooch (1972) has put forward a somewhat similar idea, only this time not based on the two sides of the brain and body, but on different structures within the brain. He comes up with the view that one structure deals mainly with the outside world – the physical, material universe – while the other deals mainly with the inner, existential universe. Again it is the rational, external, impersonal one, mainly associated with the male, that has been approved and stressed by society, and the emotional, internal, personal one, mainly associated with the female, that has been devalued.

He says that a subsystem of the 'male' structure is concerned primarily with aggression and flight, with states of rage and states of fear, while a subsystem of the 'female' structure is concerned with states of rest, of quiescence, of simple being – and also with sexual arousal. This again is a split *within* the person: we all have every one of these tendencies, played up or played down.

Now if Ornstein or Gooch is correct (and there are many other people with similar kinds of views) psychic celibacy would also be an *internal* mechanism, by means of which people cut themselves off from part of their own reality. This process would be more severe for men, though it would apply to both men and women as a general process. On this view, then, psychic celibacy would be the survival of an ancient heritage. But it would need to be broken down if men and women were to reveal their potential and avoid being limited and crippled. So this is another point of view which I think adds to its potential importance.

Implications for research

Given this kind of background, what are the implications for research in this area? It may be useful to lay the whole thing out in the form of specific questions to be asked and answered.

Is there such a thing as psychic celibacy?
What forms does it take?
How does it change?
Can I find out without becoming unauthentic?
Can I find out without alienating the subjects?
Is the project politically justifiable?
Does the project help to break down patriarchy?
Does the project do justice to the insights of a dialectical approach?
Is the research efficient in a technical sense?

The main aim of such research in terms of its scientific utility could be to establish or confute psychic celibacy as a measurable quantity, enshrined in objective scales that can then be used in other research studies, perhaps carried out by people with quite different orientations.

It seems important to note, too, that particular attention should be paid in this research to the implications for the world of work. It seems clear that there are definite connections between the general theme of male-superior/female-inferior, and the kind of dominance hierarchies commonly found in organizations of many kinds. Whatever we can discover in this research about the way in which men avoid 'female' approaches at work *even when they might be more appropriate* will be highly relevant to the current work going on to investigate such work approaches as power sharing, work democracy, quality of working life, self management, participation, and the like.

But I want to make it abundantly clear that the aims of this research are not just scientific. I want to clarify, explore, and change my own attitudes as a result of this research. I want to get each man I interview to re-examine his own attitudes, see them in a clearer light, and perhaps change them. I want the results to be used by men in their own consciousness-raising efforts. In the light of the results obtained so far, the research method, which involves setting up discussion amongst those who have been interviewed, is not a neutral, removed, distant one. I want the research methods to be considered as much as the research results. To me, this is not just about pushing the frontiers of science forward in yet another area: it is about social change.

References

ARMISTEAD, N. (ed.) (1974) *Reconstructing Social Psychology*. Harmondsworth: Penguin.

ATKINSON, T.G. (1974) *Amazon Odyssey*. New York: Link Books.

BARRY, H., BACON, M.K., and CHILD, I.L. (1957) A cross-cultural survey of some sex differences in socialization, *Journal of Abnormal and Social Psychology* 55:327-32.

BEM, S.L. (1974) The measurement of psychological androgyny. *Journal of Consulting and Clinical Psychology* 44:155-62.

BIANCHI, E.C. and REUTHER, R.R. (1976) *From Machismo to Mutuality: Essays on Sexism and Woman-Man Liberation*. Ramsey, N.J.: Paulist Press.

BROVERMAN, I.K., BROVERMAN, D.M., CLARKSON, F.E., ROSENKRANTZ, P.S., and VOGEL, S.R. (1970) Sex role stereotypes and clinical judgements of mental health. *Journal of Consulting and Clinical Psychology* 34:1-7.

BURRIS, B. *et al.* (1971) *Fourth World Manifesto*.

D'ANDRADE, R.G. (1970) Sex differences and cultural institutions. In, L. Hudson (1970).

DUBERMAN, L. (1975) *Gender and Sex in Society*. New York: Praeger Publishers.

FARRELL, W. (1975) *The Liberated Man*. London: Bantam.

GOOCH, S. (1972) *Total Man*. London: Allan Lane.

GOODMAN, A. and WALBY, P. (1975) *A Book About Men*. London: Quartet Books.

GOTTESMAN, I.I. (1963) Heritability of personality: A demonstration. *Psychological Monographs*. 77:1-21.

HARFORD, T. *et al.* (1967) Personality correlates of masculinity-femininity. *Psychological Reports* 21:881-84.

HARTLEY, R. (1959) Sex role pressures in the socialization of the male child. *Psychological Reports* 5:457-68.

HEATHER, N. (1976) *Radical Perspectives in Psychology*. London: Methuen.

HUDSON, L. (ed.) (1970) *The Ecology of Human Intelligence*. Harmondsworth: Penguin.

JEFFREYS, S. and HODSON, N. (1977) Worker control of reproduction, *Catcall* 5.

JOURARD, S. (1971) Some lethal aspects of the male role. In S. Jourard, *The Transparent Self*. Princeton: Van Nostrand.

KAGAN, J. (1964) Acquisition and significance of sex typing and sex role identity. In, M.L. Hoffman and L.W. Hoffman (eds), *Review of Child Development Research* (vol. 1), New York: Russell Sage Foundation.

KORDA, M. (1975) *Male Chauvinism*. London: Coronet.

MACCOBY, E. (ed.) (1966) *The Development of Sex Differences*. Stanford, Calif.: Stanford University Press.

MILLER, J.B. (ed.) (1973) *Psychoanalysis and Women*. Harmondsworth: Penguin.

MEAD, M. (1950) *Male and Female*. Harmondsworth: Penguin.

MURDOCK, G.P. (1937) Comparative data on the division of labour by sex. *Social Forces* 15, quoted in L. Hudson (1970).

NICHOLS, J. (1975) *Men's Liberation*. Harmondworth: Penguin.

ORNSTEIN, R. (1972) *The Psychology of Consciousness*. San Fransisco: W.II. Freeman.

ROWAN, J. (1973) *The Science of You*. London: Davis-Poynter.

——(1974) Research as intervention. In, N. Armistead (1974).

——(1975) *The Social Individual*. London: Davis-Poynter.

——(1976a) *Ordinary Ecstasy: Humanistic Psychology in Action*. London: Routledge and Kegan Paul.

——(1976b) *The Power of the Group*. London: Davis-Poynter.

SEIDENBERG, R. (1973) Is anatomy destiny? In, J.B. Miller (1973).

SEXTON, P.C. (1969) *The Feminized Male*. New York: Random House.

PART TWO

Motherhood

FOUR

The meanings of motherhood

HAYDÉE MARCOS

In the past motherhood was taken for granted, so that questions about its meaning tended not to be raised. The fact of being a woman was assumed to imply a desire for motherhood. Yet comparisons between different cultures as well as observation of women within the same culture have established that there are different ways of being a mother, and that, even before becoming one, there are various ways of experiencing the biological functions associated with procreation. ✓

The few studies that attempt to explain attitudes towards motherhood can be classified as follows. According to psychoanalysis, they originate from the process of identification with the mother that follows the 'discovery of castration' (Freud 1933). According to social learning theorists it is identification with the mother and imitation of her behaviour patterns that explain the daughter's behaviour (Uddenberg 1974). From a psycho-sociological viewpoint, attitudes towards motherhood

71

are explained in terms of the internalization of the social role prescriptions for women (Busfield 1974).

My own view about the formation of these attitudes is somewhat different. I would suggest that attitudes to motherhood are not simply determined by early experiences and that differences in the meaning that women attach to motherhood can be best understood in terms of a continuing cognitive process. In other words, by the time a woman becomes a mother her self-image incorporates not only the values and conceptualizations of her family and social group, but also her perception of the way her own personal history affects her current situation. It is this self-image that influences the meaning she will confer on motherhood and the view towards her expected child.

The research reported here concentrates on the connections between three factors: the woman's perception of her relationship with her parents, the place of motherhood in her life, and her image of the expected child.

Eighty women expecting their first baby were recruited in ante-natal sessions in public hospitals, according to the following criteria: they had to be French, raised by both parents until at least the age of fourteen, and living with the father of their expected child. These clinics had a good reputation for psychoprophylactic training during pregnancy, and this, together with the fact that the women were volunteers and not subject to any pressure from the clinic staff to participate in the research, means that the sample is biased towards middle-class women and those with relatively high levels of education. The ages of the women ranged from eighteen to thirty-seven with the majority being aged twenty-two to twenty-eight.

The women were interviewed about their expectations concerning motherhood. The interviews covered such areas as the woman's psychological state during pregnancy, when and for what reasons she had begun to want a child, the changes she expected in herself and in her relationships with those with whom she was closely involved. The aim was to encourage women to talk about their feelings concerning motherhood rather than to establish exact, 'objective' information on each of these points. In contrast to the unconscious fantasies about 'wanting a child' on which psychoanalytically-inspired writers concentrate (Freud 1933; Kestenberg 1956; Benedeck 1960; 1970), the present research deals with those aspects of motherhood that women consciously expect will change their relationships with themselves, their partner, and their wider social group. Relationships with parents were explored by means of a questionnaire, which is described later. First of all material from the interviews will be discussed.

Interview material was subjected to content analysis in which an attempt was made to keep as close as possible to the women's own conceptualizations while creating a limited number of content categories. *Table 4(1)* sets out the women's answers to the question 'When did you first decide you wanted a child?'

Table 4(1)   *When did you first decide you wanted a child? (n=80)*

Always wanted a child	26
From beginning of relationship with present partner	19
As a result of changes in own personality*	16
Never really wanted a child**	2
Other/no response	17

* Different changes have been grouped together: feeling of social integration, discovery of children at birth of nephew or niece, etc.
** The relative absence of this type of response is due to the way in which the sample was obtained.

The reasons women gave for wanting a child are set out in *Table 4(2)*. These answers compare with those reported by Flapan (1969) among pregnant women in so far as they both refer to the women's current life circumstances, only some of whom were expecting their first child.

In contrast, when students (male and female) were asked a similar question by Hoffman (1972) religious or moral reasons were mentioned that were not expressed by pregnant women in the present or in Flapan's study. This suggests that the types of reason given depend on how far the question is seen as abstract or hypothetical.

The women's responses to questions about their present psychological state were predominantly but not exclusively positive as can be seen from *Table 4(3)*.

When women were asked what changes they expected in themselves as a result of having a baby they gave the replies set out in *Table 4(4)*.

Table 4(2) *Why did you want a child?* *

Love children	18
It's an extension of the couple**	18
It's normal for a woman	15
Someone to protect/who depends on you, a little one of one's own	13
Gives an aim/meaning to life	12
Cannot imagine a childless couple**	11
To shape someone, to shape a life	11
To create emotional links	11
To reproduce happy experience of her own family	4
To please husband	3

 *   Each woman could give more than one answer.

**   Although these are similar responses, they have been separated because, if the second somehow implies the first, the converse is not true.

Table 4(3) *Present psychological state**

More assured, calmer, better	27
No change or OK	24
Tired, anxious, feelings of impotence	15
Nervous, irritable, aggressive	13
Anxious about childbirth/raising the baby	7
Feeling that the child is not part of her	2

 *   Women could give more than one answer.

Half of the women who replied to questions concerning what changes they expected in their relationship with their husband as a result of the pregnancy expected the relationship to improve, nearly one third did not expect their relationship to change, while some envisaged that it might be adversely affected because of their preoccupation with the child (see *Table 4(5)*).

Very few women expected that the birth of their child would create difficulties in their relationship with their own parents (see *Table 4(6)*).

Table 4(4) *Changes expected in herself**

No changes**	37
More assured/valued/fulfilled***	24
Will have more responsibilities	19
More responsible/calm/tolerant	17
Fear of becoming only a mother****	9
More womanly/understand mothers better	9

*	Each woman could give more than one answer.
**	There were some instances where the woman spontaneously answered in terms of changes in her relationship with her husband or parents. These are coded in *Table 4 (5)*.
***	This includes responses where the woman expects that other people will value her more.
****	These include answers such as, 'I hope not to change, to remain interested in other things than the child'.

Table 4(5) *Expected changes in woman's relationship with husband (n=67*)*

Better/stronger/even closer	27
No change	21
Fear of being preoccupied with child/'hope' that this won't happen	12
Husband more affectionate/considerate	7

*	This falls short because some women did not answer the question, or said they did not know what changes to expect. Some responses could not be coded.

Meanings of motherhood

Notions of 'adjustment' and 'maladjustment' have prevailed in studies of women's attitude to motherhood (see, for example, Zemlick and Watson 1953; Doty 1967; Nilsson *et al.* 1971; Shereshefsky and Yarrow 1973; Breen 1975). This is a simplistic conceptualization. In order to ascertain whether other configurations existed, a statistical method known as hierarchical analysis was

Table 4(6) *Expected changes in woman's relationship with her own parents (n=64*)*

No change	26
Better relationship with both**	17
Better relationship with mother**	14
Possible conflicts about the baby	7

*   Some answers could not be coded. Other women either did not answer the question or said they did not know what changes to expect.

**   These group together those responses indicating an even greater closeness than already existed and those expecting an improvement in relationships that were currently not particularly good.

applied to the interview material. The programme for the method used here derives from factorial correspondences analysis (Benzécri 1976). As a result five distinct configurations of themes can be seen, which because of their content have been called 'fears', 'self-assertion', 'maternal identification', 'expectations centred on the child', and 'development' (see *Table 4* (7) below).

Three of these configurations are composed entirely of optimistic themes, i.e. three groups of subjects assign a positive meaning to motherhood. Of the other two configurations, 'self-assertion' contains both positive and negative themes, while 'fears' contains negative themes only.

No general conclusions may be drawn from the fact that only one group assigns exclusively negative meaning to motherhood. The population in this study is biased, being composed mainly of women who positively desired or at least happily accepted their pregnancies, hence the preponderance of 'optimistic' responses. It will be necessary to study a wider population if a more sophisticated analysis of negative meanings is to be carried out.

In two of the positive configurations, 'Maternal identification' and 'Development', motherhood is viewed as improving the woman's status and her own and others' perceptions of her. The third positive configuration, 'Expectations centred on the child', focuses on the fulfilment of the woman's desire for a child.

The complex of themes labelled 'Maternal identification' seems to indicate that the maternal role is perceived, by this

76

Table 4(7) *Configuration of themes (n=80)*

Fears (n=15)

Present state	Tired, anxious, feeling of impotence. Feeling that the child is not part of her.
Expected changes	Fear of becoming only a mother. Fear that preoccupation with child will affect relationship with child's father.

Self-assertion (n=18)

Motivation for having a child	It's normal for a woman. It's an extension of the couple. To shape someone, to shape a life. To create emotional links.
Present state	Nervous, irritable, aggressive Anxious about childbirth or raising the new-born. Anxious about abnormal child.
Expected changes	More sure, more valued, more fulfilled. More womanly, understand mothers better. More responsible, more calm, more tolerant. Better, stronger relationship with husband. No change in relationship with parents.

Maternal identification (n=16)

Time since which she has wanted a child	Has always wanted a child.
Expected changes	Husband more affectionate, more considerate.

Has already had experience with children	Better relationship with mother.

Expectations centred on the child (n=12)

Motivation for having a child	Cannot imagine a childless couple. Loves children. Someone to protect, a little one of one's own, someone who depends on you.
Present state	No change or OK.
Expected changes	Better relationship with both parents.

Development (n=19)

Time since which she has wanted a child	Existence of partnership with child's father.
Motivation for having a child	Gives an aim, gives meaning to life.
Present state	More assured, calmer, better.
Expected changes	Will enter adults' world. Will have more responsibilities.

---

group of women, as being a component of their sense of self identity (has 'always' wished for a child). This complex also includes an item of the factual type: 'experience with children'. This has been noted whenever a woman has had lasting contacts with children before her pregnancy, within her family or profession. Where these contacts result from a vocational choice (nanny, teacher, etc.) the presence of 'motherliness' (Deutsch 1945) long before pregnancy seems probable. Other instances are mainly eldest daughters having helped their mother with younger siblings. Nilsson *et al.* (1971) note a correlation between having been an eldest daughter and identification with the mother (by 'identification' he means the likeness of a woman's self-image and the image she gives of her parents). He also assumes that identification correlates with a life-long wish to be a mother. Thus, in his study, two of the 'maternal identification' class components are associated with a third variable. And one may assume that the latter, 'identification with mother', is related to what we call 'maternal identification'. What I mean by this term is not identification with one's own mother but rather with the maternal roles or mothers generally. But it seems probable that the likeness of a woman's self-image with the image of her mother is partly a result of attributing motherly qualities to herself as well as to her mother (this unfortunately remains an assumption as Nilsson does not, in his paper, give the content of these images).

The item 'greater closeness to the mother' in many cases means that the woman now feels she is like her mother, has more in common with her, and can talk with her more freely. In other instances the subject thinks that her mother's perception of her has changed.

For women in the second positive configuration, 'Development', motherhood apparently represents the passage to a new stage of life, a maturity originating from the partnership with the child's father (has wanted a child 'since the partnership has existed'). Here the meaning of motherhood appears rather clearly in the expected changes. As to the items relevant to present state and motivations for having a child, they show a feeling of having come to terms with oneself. Thus motherhood is here perceived as an adult role: the subject feels able to play it and to gain access to the adult world.

Some authors, mainly Bibring (1959) and Breen (1975) have assumed that motherhood may actually represent a stage in the development of the personality. Developing our approach, as we do, within the context of the *women's* vision it is possible to avoid the methodological and conceptual difficulties raised by such an assumption.

The final positive configuration, 'Expectations centred on child', comprises views of motherhood that attach more importance to the presence of the child than to the effect that motherhood may have upon the woman's sense of self-identity (see 'Motivations' and 'Present state').

The 'Self-assertion' configuration encompasses a complexity of themes both positive and negative. Motherhood seems for the subjects within this class to be a creative task (to shape a life, to shape somebody, to create emotional links), the achievement of which may give rise to an increased feeling of self-worth. The women in this group also see 'motherhood' resulting in a 'better, stronger relationship with husband'.

The response 'It's normal for a woman' does not apparently mean an identification between motherhood and womanhood. It is interesting to note its rather stable association, throughout various analyses, with the response 'irritable, nervous, aggressive'. The two themes seem to express an attitude of self-assertion towards the psychologist during the interview. Mention of feeling 'irritable, aggressive' is the opposite of mentioning a depressive state (tired, anxious, feeling of impotence) which belongs to the 'fears' class.

The entirely negative configuration of themes has been called 'Fears'. These fears revolve around the perception that motherhood will have an impoverishing effect upon the individual life of the woman and upon the marriage relationship.

It seems worth noting that this analysis results in a clear distinction between two types of anxiety – the one that we have titled 'fears' described above and the other, subsumed under 'Self-assertion', which comprises anxieties concerned with the woman's own capacity of coping with childbirth (its real and fantasied risks) and the early relationship with the child. 'Fears' comprises those relevant to a less rich individual life and partnership. The presence of fears in the 'self-assertion' class may be better understood when one examines how the women within these groups describe their relationship with their own mothers (see below).

In summary, it has been possible to outline a variety of positive and negative themes relating to motherhood and to move away from the conceptualization of adjustment and maladjustment as the best way of understanding women's attitudes to motherhood.

The meanings that women attach to the birth of a first child are the result of highly complex experiences. Nevertheless a woman's perception of her relationship with her own parents seems particularly relevant. Primarily, and this has often been stated (Freud 1933; Deutsch 1945; Rheingold 1964; Racamier 1967; Nilsson *et al.* 1971; Breen 1975), basic identification with maternal figures is important. And yet motherhood cannot sim-

80

ply be reduced to this. It is a creative process, and specific to each woman since after the birth she will be confronted with a being who is in some senses a double of herself.

Therefore, her feeling of self-worth as an individual and as a woman appear central. They underlie her confidence in her own creative capacity and her more-or-less assured acceptance of this other self that will be created. Moreover her perception of her relationship with her parents – e.g. whether she feels loved by them or not, whether she is dependent, etc. – plays an essential part in a woman's feeling of her own worth. And, likewise, the perception of the self as a valid and autonomous being intervenes in yet another aspect of motherhood. Becoming a mother constitutes a transition to a new stage of the life-cycle, in so far as it implies responsibility for shaping a new human being as well as taking on new relationships both with the baby and with the woman's partner, all of which place heavy emotional demands on the woman.

Relationship with parents

A woman's relationship with her parents was explored by means of a questionnaire. The same forty-four questions were put once about the mother and once about the father. Four further questions asked how well she got on, during childhood and adolescence, with her mother as compared with her father. Here are a few examples:

> Do you think your mother's (father's) disposition was compatible with your own? (Highly compatible, fairly, moderately, not very, incompatible.)

> When you did something she (he) didn't like, did she (he) seem unhappy? (Very often, often, sometimes, seldom, never.)

> Did you feel a preference for one of your parents? (A marked preference for father, a slight preference, no preference, a slight preference for mother, a marked preference for mother.)

There were also open-ended questions aimed at amplifying certain closed ones. Factor analysis of the questionnaire answers brings out two main factors: good/bad relationship and proximity/distance. Two bipolar variables have been constructed from

81

those items that correlated more strongly with the factors. Each of these variables divides the population into two groups of approximately equal size. The first of these contains items concerning mutual understanding between the woman and each parent and the compatibility of her temperament with theirs. Proximity/distance contains items to do with emotional dependence between the woman and her parents (for more details see Marcos in press). It is not possible in the short space available to analyse the relationship between these two variables nor their specific influence on the woman's perception of motherhood. These have been presented in a drastically shortened way and can only serve as indicators. With these reservations in mind it is still possible to relate the woman's perception of her relationship with her parents to the way in which she approaches motherhood.

Distance/proximity

Motherhood as 'self-assertion' is considerably more frequent in women who have felt particularly protected or watched over by their parents than among women who report a certain emotional distance between their parents and themselves. The latter are more likely to approach motherhood with their expectations centred on the child.

It seems that when a woman considers that she was not highly valued by her parents and indeed somewhat 'crushed' by them she seeks a sense of personal worth in becoming a mother herself and yet is simultaneously unsure of her ability to cope with the task. These problems are absent among women for whom the image of motherhood means essentially the presence of a child. Women whose mothers enabled them to be autonomous constitute the majority (66 per cent) of women whose expectations were centred on the child.

Good/bad relationship with parents

A high proportion of the women in the 'Maternal identification' group report having had a poor relationship with their father and a good one with their mother.

Women who see themselves as misunderstood or not supported by both parents constitute a high proportion (73 per cent) of those who expect motherhood to bring problems ('Fears' group).

None of the women who report having had a good relationship with both parents are to be found in the 'Fears' category.

Those women who had a good relationship with both parents are particularly likely to approach motherhood in an optimistic way and specifically to form a large proportion of the 'Expectations centred on the child' group.

The present study shows that, when analysing the concomitants of women's attitudes to motherhood, it is necessary to consider their relationship not only with their mother but also with their father. This finding is in contrast to those studies that suggest that identification with a 'good mother' is a necessary and sufficient condition for 'adjustment' to motherhood. In any case material reported earlier in this paper has drawn attention to the limitations of an 'adjustment' model for an understanding of women's attitudes towards motherhood.

References

BENEDECK, T. (1960) The organization of the reproductive drive. *International Journal of Psycho-analysis* **51** (1):1-15.

—— (1970) Psychobiology of pregnancy. In, E.J. Anthony and T. Benedeck (eds), *Parenthood*. Boston: Little, Brown and Co.

BENZÉCRI, J.P. (1976) *L'Analyse des Données*. Paris: Dunod.

BIBRING, G. (1959) Some considerations of the psychological processes in pregnancy. *Psychoanalytical Study of the Child* **14**:113-21.

BREEN, D. (1975) *The Birth of a First Child*. London: Tavistock Publications.

BUSFIELD, J. (1974) Ideologies and reproduction. In, P.M. Martin and J.J. Richard (eds), *The Integration of the Child into a Social World*. New York: Cambridge University Press.

DEUTSCH, H. (1945) *The Psychology of Woman*. New York: Grune and Stratton.

DOTY, B. (1967) Relationships among attitudes in pregnancy and other maternal characteristics. *The Journal of Genetic Psychology* **111**:203-17.

FLAPAN, N. (1969) A paradigm for the analysis of childbearing motivations. *American Journal of Orthopsychiatry* **39**(3):402-7.

FREUD, S. (1933) *The Psychology of woman. New Introductory Lectures in Psychoanalysis* (vol.22, Standard Edition). London: Hogarth Press.

HOFFMAN, L. (1972) A psychological perspective on the value of children to parents: concepts and measures. In, J.T. Fawcett (ed.), *Satisfactions and Costs of Children: Theories, Concepts and Methods*. Honolulu: East-West Center.

KESTENBERG, J. (1956). On the development of maternal feelings in early childhood. *Psychoanalytical Study of the Child* **11**:257-91.

MARCOS, H. (in press) L'adulte et ses parents: une étude d'images chez la femme enceinte. *Journal International de Psychologie Appliquée.*

NILSSON, A., UDDENBERG, N., and ALMGREN, P. (1971) Parental relations and identification in women with special regard to para-natal emotional adjustment. *Acta Psychiatrica Scandinavica* **47**, 57-81.

RACAMIER, P. (1976). Troubles de la sexualité féminine et du sens maternel. *Bulletin Officiel de la Société Francaise de psychoprophylaxie obstétricale* **432**:1-40.

RHEINGOLD, J.C. (1964) *The Fear of Being a Woman.* New York: Grune and Stratton (cited in Nilsson *et al.*, 1971).

SHERESHEFSKY, P. and YARROW, L. (1973) *Psychological Aspects of a First Pregnancy and Early Postnatal Adaptation.* New York: Raven Press.

UDDENBERG, N. (1974) Reproductive adaptation in mother and daughter. *Acta Psychiatrica Scandinavica* **51** (Suppl. no. 254).

ZEMLICK, M.J. and WATSON, D. (1953) Maternal attitudes of acceptance and rejection during and after pregnancy. *American Journal of Orthopsychiatry* **23**:570-84.

FIVE

Self-perceptions during pregnancy and early motherhood

EVA ZAJICEK

Erikson (1963) describes the human life cycle as a progressive development between birth and death through a series of transitions from one growth stage to another. He believes that the essential ingredients for healthy transition into adulthood are choice, change, and commitment, and the means by which such transition is said to occur are via free role experimentation and crisis (Erikson 1963). The beliefs underlying this theory of development are that the individual should be free to choose and modify his/her own destiny, and that where such choice is possible he/she will always move in a positive, self-enhancing direction (Goldstein 1940; Rogers 1961).

There are some situations, however, where free role experimentation is not always possible. Commitment to a task or role can occur without experimentation and choice, especially when the individual is brought up to believe that his or her destiny lies within a particular situation. For many women this is the case with the role of motherhood. They are brought up to expect and to believe that they will become mothers and that, in doing so, they may have to sacrifice, at least temporarily, other roles and tasks to which they may feel drawn. This situation exists because, within the main cycle of human development, they go through another cycle, which is that of reproductive development. This cycle begins with menstruation, ends with menopause, and has as its climax the transition to motherhood. The female cycle of development into adulthood nevertheless goes through a series of transitions common to both sexes, such as leaving school, getting a job, and getting married, but it is almost always linked with and directed towards a point of fulfilment that is seen to be the first pregnancy and birth of the child.

In an elaboration of Erikson's theories, Marcia (1966) suggested that individuals who commit themselves before or instead of a period of free role experimentation (a situation that Marcia calls foreclosure), may be less mature and less fulfilled than those who have achieved their identities *because of* such experimentation. However, Marcia and Friedman (1970) have shown a difference between men and women in so far as women are more secure with themselves and less anxious within a foreclosure situation than in a crisis one. It may be that there are intrinsic differences between men and women and that women are as content with having a role prescribed for them as they would be if they sought out their own. It may also be that women have a basic need to become mothers and that therefore the role of motherhood is a natural path for them. A number of early theoreticians attempted to substantiate this particular view by stressing that women's main fulfilment occurs when they accept and commit themselves to the role of motherhood (Freud 1933; Deutsch 1947; Rheingold 1964). Such theories argued that women have one role, and motherhood has one universal meaning: '[woman] is a passive, dependent person whose only or chief role is mothering, and childbearing represents fulfilment of her biologically determined purpose in life' (summarized by Grimm 1969:129). However, as opposed to this view, it has been suggested that the conditioning process is such that many women are forced into the motherhood role regardless of their own needs, and that whilst some may respond positively to this and feel content with a choice that they would have made anyway, others may feel resentful about being in a situation that they would not have chosen and which is intrinsically frustrating to their own needs (Rossi 1968; Friedan 1963).

Women's reactions towards pregnancy and motherhood have been the focus of some attention during the last fifty years. Research on the first pregnancy experiences has shown that many women do not actually plan to become pregnant (Hall and Mohr 1933; Breen 1975), experience some negative feelings when they discover that they are pregnant (Caplan 1960; Nash 1973), and become anxious and depressed during the pregnancy (Thompson 1942; Curtis 1955; Bibring 1959; Breen 1975). This is hardly the picture of sublime contentment that the earlier theories would have predicted. Erikson's (1963) emphasis on the 'normal developmental crises' of life has been used by recent theoreticians to interpret the conflicts in terms of the normal crisis that occurs with the transition into a new life stage, the resolution of which will result in development: 'As it is now taken for granted that psychological disturbance is typical of the adolescent person, it is proposed to accept in the same way that there is a disturbance peculiar to the period of pregnancy arising from emotional, physiological or social stress inherent in the pregnancy period' (Bibring 1959:119). This led to a theoretical model that encompassed the conflicts of the pregnancy period whilst still maintaining the old view that motherhood is a positive developmental experience for women. As Chertok said: 'Development through conflict . . . constitutes the ground on which every woman elaborates the pattern of her motherhood'. (1966:30).

Such a view led to a fresh emphasis on the possibility of the attainment of maturity, identity, and an increase in self-esteem as a result of motherhood (Bardwick 1971; Shainess 1963; Racamier 1961; Pines 1972). It was regarded as important for the attainment of this development, and for the successful establishment of a good mother-child relationship, that the conflicts of pregnancy should be resolved before the birth of the child (Bibring 1959). However, the research studies that have examined women's reactions during the early maternal years have not come up with much evidence to suggest that the crisis of maternity is magically resolved once the child has been born. Social research has shown that many couples experience a marital crisis after the birth of the first child (Le Masters 1957; Hobbs 1965). Many women experience a mild form of depression ('maternity

87

blues') in the first two weeks after the delivery (Pitt 1968), and about a third of women seem to continue with depressive problems for some months after the birth (Pleshette *et al.* 1956; Blair *et al.* 1970). Women bringing up young children have been described as less satisfied and more stressed than women without children (Campbell *et al.* 1976). Such findings tend to support the idea that, on the whole, motherhood is not a particularly enhancing experience for many women. In fact, Friedan (1963) suggested that it might be a period of negative identity, which consists of being unsure of whom one is and feeling a lack of confidence, and Rossi (1968) pointed out that many women actually lose ground in personal development and self esteem during the maternal years.

Considering the large number of contradictory views and emotional responses to this issue it seems important to study the specific effects of pregnancy and early motherhood on women's perceptions of themselves. Self esteem is an important dimension of identity and it has been consistently referred to in both a positive and negative sense in relation to the transition to motherhood. An individual's personal evaluation of herself is said to be crucial in affecting her relationships with others (Berger 1952) and her general adjustment (Raimy 1948). It is for these reasons that I have chosen to focus on women's self-esteem during their transition to motherhood.

Method

This paper describes one part of an ongoing longitudinal study of mothers and babies being carried out by the Family Research Unit in an Inner London Borough. During the course of one year all British born women of sixteen and over who were having their first baby were interviewed when they booked at the antenatal clinics of the London Hospital. They were approximately two months pregnant at the time. The main aim of this interview was to select three samples of women who could be followed up at later stages. The samples were made up of married, cohabiting, and single women. The aim of the main study is to trace the development of the child and mother-child relationships from the time of early pregnancy to when the child is of school age. A small sample of women was selected from the main study for the purpose of this present investigation. Information specific to self-concept and self-esteem was obtained from fifty-six women from the larger study.

The women were seen in their homes at seven months of pregnancy and four months and fourteen months after the birth of the child. At these times they were interviewed at length about their current life situation and their expectations, attitudes, and satisfaction with new role and circumstances. They were also questioned about their health, both physical and psychological, after the birth, and about child problems, child behaviour, and the child's temperamental characteristics.

Self-esteem measure

The women were given two identical semantic differential checklists to fill in at each stage (Wylie 1974), on which they were asked to rate themselves in terms of self and ideal self on a seven-point scale over thirty different dimensions. The dimensions that were used had been elicited from mothers in descriptions of themselves, close friends, and close relatives in a previous pilot study. They included:

    quick tempered – even tempered
    sympathetic – unsympathetic
    contented – discontented
    motherly – not motherly
    responsible – irresponsible
    friendly – unfriendly
    humpy – placid

An indication of self-esteem was taken to be the discrepancy between a woman's rating on the self scale and on the ideal scale on any given characteristic. It indicated operationally the degree to which she valued the state that she described herself as being in. The total discrepancy between self and ideal over all the dimensions gave a general index of self-esteem (Rogers 1961). So for each woman, in addition to the information obtained from the interviews, a self-esteem score was obtained in pregnancy, and at four months and fourteen months after the birth.

Emotional difficulties

At each stage the women were questioned extensively about

emotional difficulties. These were assessed from a standardized psychiatric interview designed by Rutter and his colleagues (1976) at the Institute of Psychiatry. A definite emotional difficulty was operationally defined as the presence of emotional symptoms of a severity that produced impairment of daily functioning and relationships in the woman's life. A mild emotional difficulty was defined as the presence of emotional symptoms that were not severe enough to produce any impairment in her behaviour or relationships.

Description of the sample

AGE

At the time of the main pregnancy interview (in the last trimester of pregnancy) the mean age of the mothers was 22.05 years. Fifteen (27 per cent) were under twenty years old.

CLASS

All the women came from working-class backgrounds. That is, their fathers had been employed in occupations classed according to the Registrar General's classifications, as III (non-manual) and below.

MARITAL STATUS

At the time of the main pregnancy interview: thirty-eight (68 per cent) were married; five (9 per cent) were cohabiting; thirteen (23 per cent) were single (two were divorced).

By fourteen months after the birth, two of the married women had separated from their husbands, and four of the single women were married.

Results

EMOTIONAL DIFFICULTIES

At every stage the symptoms were predominantly those of depression with associated anxiety.

(The totals differ at each stage because information was not obtained from every woman each time, either because she

Table 5(1) *The incidence of emotional difficulties during and after pregnancy.*

	7 months pregnant	4 months postpartum	14 months postpartum
No emotional difficulties	36 (64%)	31 (57%)	35 (70%)
Mild emotional difficulties	9 (16%)	17 (31%)	7 (14%)
Definite emotional difficulties	11 (19%)	6 (11%)	8 (16%)
	56	54	50

refused to co-operate, or because the presence of another person at the time of the interview meant that the interviewer could not carry out extensive personal questioning. This situation exists with reference to all the results presented in this paper. At each stage there were questions that were not asked of some women. Often it was a result of the fact that their husbands were present at the time of the interview.)

In pregnancy a total of 35 per cent of the women had some emotional symptoms. At four months after the birth 42 per cent of the women were experiencing symptoms. Half of these women had also had symptoms during pregnancy. At fourteen months after the birth 30 per cent of the women had emotional symptoms; 87 per cent of these women had also had problems either at pregnancy or at four months after the birth. It would seem that there is a high degree of continuity of emotional difficulties over time, for the period being studied. Overall there is no significant difference between the proportions of women who became depressed at each stage; however, it can be seen that the slightly higher frequency of problems at four months is largely due to an increase in mild emotional symptoms at that time. These findings give support to the notion that the first few months after the birth are a time for potential 'blues' (Pitt 1968).

MAJOR MILESTONES

In order to assess whether pregnancy was regarded as an important life event by the women, they were asked to describe the major milestones that had affected them in the past, and to assess the comparative effects of pregnancy upon them.

The most common milestones that were mentioned were the beginning of the relationship with husband or present boyfriend (mentioned by twenty-three women), parental changes such as deaths, illness, major rows, or breakups (mentioned by seventeen women), and changes in occupation or leaving school (mentioned by nine women). Only four of the women thought that pregnancy was a major milestone. However, thirty of the women felt that they had been changed by pregnancy. The sorts of changes that the women described were as follows:

'It's what I've always wanted, I'm very happy.'
'It was very exciting at first, but it's such a long time to wait.'
'It fits in very well, I feel good.'
'It's the next best thing to marriage.'
'It gives me more interest in the future.'
'It's made me more mature – more grown up, more responsible.'
'It's a wonderful thing in life.'
'It's helped me to understand more.'
'It's great, I've got something of my own at last.'
'It's made me very hard.'
'I worry about the baby instead of myself.'

SELF-ESTEEM SCORES

Table 5(2) *Self esteem scores across time (higher scores indicate lower self-esteem)*

	Mean	Standard deviation	Number
Pregnancy	10.39	4.36	56
4 months	10.79	4.63	51
14 months	9.57	4.2	49

A total self-ideal discrepancy was obtained for each woman at each stage. This is an index of self-esteem, with high discrepancy being indicative of low self-esteem, and low discrepancy being indicative of high self-esteem. *Table 5(2)* shows the mean self-esteem scores for the whole group at the three different stages. There is no significant difference between the means.

Figure 5(1) Correlations of self-esteem scores over time: Main study (n = 56)

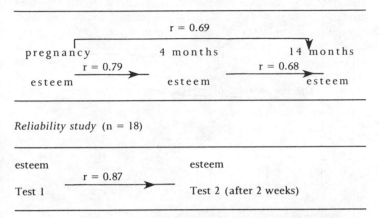

Reliability study (n = 18)

Figure 5(1) shows the results of correlations of the self-esteem scores across the three periods of time (pregnancy to four months, four months to fourteen months, pregnancy to fourteen months). They are all significant at the .001 level.

A test-retest study was carried out on a separate group of eighteen mothers. They were given the two checklists twice, with a two-week interval in between. The correlation of Test 1 with Test 2 over the two weeks was 0.87. This was not significantly different from the correlation obtained between pregnancy and fourteen months in the main study.

Thus it can be said that self-esteem, as measured in this situation, does not change significantly between pregnancy, four months, and fourteen months after the birth, for this group of women. It seemed possible that, whilst the group as a whole did not change in any significant way between pregnancy and fourteen months after the birth, women with different levels of self-esteem might be affected in different ways by the experience of maternity. The women were ordered according to their self-esteem during pregnancy and split into three equal groups according to whether they were in the top, middle, or bottom of the hierarchy. The three groups have been labelled high, middle, and low self-esteem scorers.

Figure 5(2) shows the development of self esteem in the three groups across time. It can be seen that the women who had high

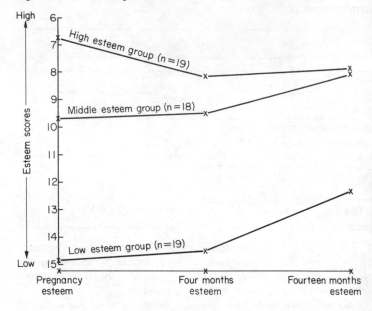

Figure 5(2) Development of self-esteem

self-esteem during pregnancy changed to a lower level between pregnancy and four months. This change is significant at the .05 level. They then remained at a fairly constant level between four months and fourteen months.

Women who had middle self-esteem during pregnancy remained unchanged throughout the time period being studied. By fourteen months there was very little difference in the self-esteem scores of those who started out with high esteem and those who started out with medium esteem.

Women with low esteem during pregnancy changed little between pregnancy and four months but did get more positive about themselves between four and fourteen months (significant at .05). However at fourteen months they were still significantly lower in self-esteem compared with the other two groups.

The information obtained from the interviews was examined to see what factors, if any, were interacting with self-esteem during pregnancy.

Table 5(3) shows the interaction between self-esteem during

Table 5(3) *Self-esteem in pregnancy and other pregnancy circumstances*

Situation as described in pregnancy	High esteem in pregnancy	Medium esteem in pregnancy	Low esteem in pregnancy	Significance
Size of family > 2 siblings	$\frac{8}{19}$ (42%)	$\frac{13}{16}$ (81%)	$\frac{15}{19}$ (79%)	<.02
Smoking history = Never smoked	$\frac{11}{18}$ (61%)	$\frac{2}{17}$ (12%)	$\frac{3}{16}$ (19%)	<.01
Emotional difficulties	$\frac{1}{19}$ (5%)	$\frac{6}{18}$ (33%)	$\frac{13}{19}$ (68%)	<.01
Uncontrollable diet change	$\frac{4}{19}$ (21%)	$\frac{10}{18}$ (55%)	$\frac{12}{19}$ (63%)	<.05
Sickness beyond 1st trimester	$\frac{4}{19}$ (21%)	$\frac{2}{18}$ (11%)	$\frac{9}{19}$ (47%)	<.05
Unwanted pregnancy	$\frac{2}{18}$ (11%)	$\frac{6}{18}$ (33%)	$\frac{10}{19}$ (53%)	<.05

pregnancy and the situation as reported at that time. High self-esteem women came from smaller families, and more often described themselves as non-smokers. Low self-esteem women were more depressed, had more uncontrollable diet change, and had more sickness. An assessment of not wanting the pregnancy was made if the woman said that she did not plan it and if her initial reaction to it was negative. More of the women with low self-esteem did not want the pregnancy.

There was one other way in which the women with low self-esteem differed from the other two groups during pregnancy. Seventy per cent of the high esteem women mentioned the beginning of the present relationship with the husband when asked to describe major milestones in their past. This was the case for 61 per cent of the middle esteem women but for only 27 per cent of the low esteem women. Women with low self-esteem, therefore, who are married and who have a stable relationship, tend not to

95

feel that the relationship has had an important effect on their lives. The differences between the groups were not a result of more of the single women being in the low self-esteem group because this was not the case. During pregnancy the single women tended to be distributed fairly evenly between the high, middle, and low self-esteem categories.

Direct questions about the relationship with the husband and the husband's involvement in the pregnancy did not reveal differences between the groups. It could be that the question about major milestones was a more subtle index of the marital relationship, and it could also be that high self-esteem and medium self-esteem women get positive reinforcement of esteem through the relationship with their husbands and that this is not the case with low self-esteem women. In order to look at this further the three groups of women were compared at four months after the birth of the child.

Table 5(4) *Pregnancy self-esteem compared with circumstances four months postpartum*

Situation at four months	High esteem in pregnancy	Medium esteem in pregnancy	Low esteem in pregnancy	Significance
Little conversation with husband*	$\frac{3}{16}$ (19%)	$\frac{5}{14}$ (35%)	$\frac{10}{13}$ (77%)	$<.01$
Dissatisfaction with conversation	$\frac{3}{15}$ (20%)	$\frac{2}{13}$ (15%)	$\frac{8}{12}$ (67%)	$<.05$
Dissatisfaction with life generally	$\frac{2}{16}$ (13%)	$\frac{5}{14}$ (36%)	$\frac{12}{17}$ (71%)	$<.01$

* Partners of women who were cohabiting at the time are here referred to as husbands.

At four months after the birth the women who had low self-esteem in pregnancy were not significantly more likely than the women in the other two groups to be depressed. However, the low self-esteem women did differ from the others in three ways. They were more likely to describe little conversation with their husbands and they were more likely to be dissatisfied about the amount of conversation that there was between themselves and their husbands. They were also more dissatisfied with life in general than the other two groups. At this stage there was no significant difference between women with high and middle self-esteem.

The situation at fourteen months for the three groups again showed differences between the high and middle self-esteem groups compared with the low self-esteem women. *Table 5(5)* shows the relationship between self-esteem during pregnancy and circumstances fourteen months after the birth.

An assessment of the types of problem each woman experienced in coping with the child was obtained by combining a number of interrelated variables: irritability with child, feelings of loss of control with the child, frequent feelings of not being able to cope, frequent visits to GP with child, dissatisfaction in looking after the child. The women who had a low self-esteem in pregnancy had a higher *non-coping score* at fourteen months.

A *dissatisfaction score* was defined as the total number of

Table 5(5) *Pregnancy self-esteem compared to circumstances fourteen months postpartum*

Situation at 14 months	High esteem in pregnancy	Medium esteem in pregnancy	Low esteem in pregnancy	Significance
Problems coping with child	$\frac{7}{17}$ (41%)	$\frac{7}{16}$ (44%)	$\frac{13}{15}$ (87%)	$<.02$
Dissatisfied with life	$\frac{2}{13}$ (15%)	$\frac{1}{11}$ (9%)	$\frac{7}{11}$ (64%)	$<.05$
Depressed	$\frac{2}{16}$ (13%)	$\frac{3}{15}$ (20%)	$\frac{10}{17}$ (59%)	$<.01$
Problems in relationship or no relationship	$\frac{4}{14}$ (29%)	$\frac{4}{13}$ (31%)	$\frac{12}{14}$ (86%)	$<.01$
High stress	$\frac{5}{16}$ (31%)	$\frac{6}{15}$ (40%)	$\frac{12}{14}$ (86%)	$<.05$
Child sleeping in parents' room	$\frac{3}{15}$ (20%)	$\frac{6}{16}$ (37%)	$\frac{12}{16}$ (75%)	$<.01$

expressed dissatisfactions in response to questions about baby, husband, and new life situation in general. The low self-esteem women were much more dissatisfied with life in every way: more depressed and also more likely to have marital problems if they were married, or to have no relationship at all.

A *stress score* was assessed from extensive questioning about the woman's situation over the fourteen months since she had had the child. Areas covered included housing, money, work, relationships, partings, deaths, and other life events. The women of low self-esteem during pregnancy reported more stresses after the birth.

The one other factor that differentiated the low self-esteem group was the fact that the child was still sleeping in the same room as the parents.

Discussion

Becoming a mother is generally regarded as an important transitional stage in the female life cycle. It has been suggested that women go through major self-concept re-evaluation during this time, but there is some disagreement as to whether it is a positive developmental phase or a negative traumatic experience. Common sense would suggest that the way in which women cope with motherhood, and the effects that it has upon them, will vary according to whether or not they welcome the experience. The findings presented in this paper tend to substantiate this view. The results suggest that becoming a mother is not of itself the sort of experience that will provoke major self-esteem re-evaluations. The group of women who were studied did not become significantly more positive or more negative about themselves between pregnancy and fourteen months after the birth. In addition, they did not become significantly more or less depressed during the same period. Quite a sizable proportion of women did experience some emotional symptoms during pregnancy, but the incidence rate did not change significantly as a result of motherhood.

The self-perceptions of the women during pregnancy had important effects upon their development after the birth, and the women who had difficulties in coping with the experience of motherhood were those who had low self-esteem during the pregnancy period. These women were the ones who did not want to be pregnant and they seemed to experience more psychological and physical problems during that time. After the birth the women who had low self-esteem during pregnancy were experiencing more problems in their relationships with their husbands and they seemed to be much more dissatisfied with their lives than the other two groups. They were also experiencing more problems in coping with the child and in making the general readjustments that are necessary for successful adaptation to the role of motherhood. Women who had low self-esteem during pregnancy did not change in their self-perceptions during the first few months of motherhood, but by the end of the first year their self-evaluations did rise significantly. However, the problems that these women were experiencing did not become less as their esteem rose, and they were still significantly more negative in their self-evaluations than the other two groups.

The findings suggest that some women enter into the role of motherhood regardless of, rather than because of, their own needs. They find themselves in a new situation that they resent because they did not choose it, and they therefore have great difficulties in coping with it. It has been suggested that the importance of any experience for an individual will depend on that person's perceptions of the experience and her perceptions of herself within that experience (Snygg and Combs 1949). People normally strive for consistency and in doing so select experiences that are not at odds with their perceptions of themselves (Lecky 1945). The cost to an individual of being in a situation that is inconsistent with her needs must be great, since she will be required to make major adaptations to reconcile the inconsistencies, or construct major defences to deny them. I would suggest that the women who feel that the role of motherhood is at odds with their view of themselves are those who have low self-esteem during pregnancy. It is impossible to say whether they are in the situation because their lack of self-esteem made them powerless to avoid it, or whether their low self-esteem is purely a function of their being in that situation. It is difficult to talk about cause and effect where so many factors are inextricably linked together. But perhaps the importance of probing into the antecedents of self-esteem is not crucial in this situation. Suffice it to say that not all women approach prospective motherhood with feelings of pleasure and fulfilment. Low self-esteem during the pregnancy period is an indication of troubles ahead. Those who feel concerned to help women cope with the not always tranquil experiences of early motherhood should be aware of this fact.

Acknowledgement

The work being done by the Family Research Unit has been generously supported by a grant from the Medical Research Council.

References

BARDWICK, J. (1971) *Pschology of Women: A Study of Bio-cultural Conflicts*. New York: Harper and Row.

BERGER, E.M. (1952) The relationship between expressed acceptance of self and expressed acceptance of others. *Journal of Abnormal and Social Psychology* **47**:778-82.

BIBRING, G. (1959) Some considerations of the psychological processes in pregnancy. *Psychoanalytic Study of the Child* **14**:113-21.

BLAIR, R.A., GILMORE, J.S., PLAYFAIR, M.R., TISDALL, M.W., and O'SHEA, C. (1970). Puerperal depression – A study of predictive factors. *Journal of the Royal College of Practitioners* **19**:22.

BREEN, D. (1975) *The Birth of a First Child*. London: Tavistock Publications.

CAMPBELL, A., CONVERSE, P.E., and RODGERS, W.L. (1976) *The Quality of American Life: Perceptions, Evaluations, and Satisfaction*. New York: Russel Sage Foundation.

CAPLAN, G. (1960) Emotional implications of pregnancy and influences on family relationships. In, H.C. Stuart and D.G. Prugh (eds), *The Healthy Child*. Cambridge, Mass.: Harvard.

CHERTOK, L. (1966) *Motherhood and Personality*. London: Tavistock Publications.

CURTIS, D. (1955) *The Normal Prenatal Patient's attitude to pregnancy*. New York: Millbank Memorial Fund.

DEUTSCH, H. (1947) *The Psychology of Women* (vol. 2). London: Research Books Ltd.

ERIKSON, E.M. (1963) *Childhood and Society* (2nd ed.). New York: Norton.

FREUD, S. (1933) The Psychology of Women. In, *New Introductory Lectures in Psychoanalysis* (vol. 22, standard edition). London: Hogarth Press.

FRIEDAN, B. (1963) *The Feminine Mystique*. London: Victor Gollancz.

GOLDSTEIN, K. (1940) *Human Nature in the light of Psychopathology*. Cambridge, Mass.: Harvard.

GRIMM, E.R. (1969) Women's attitudes and reactions to childbirth. In,

G.D. Goldman and D.S. Milman (eds), *Modern Woman:* 129-51. Springfield, Ill.: Charles. C. Thomas.

HALL, D.E. and MOHR, G.J. (1933) Prenatal attitudes of primiparae. *Marital Hygiene* 17:226-34.

HOBBS, D.F. (1965) Parenthood as crisis: a third study. *Journal of Marriage and the Family* 27(3): 367-72.

LECKY, P. (1945) *Self-consistency: A Theory of Personality.* New York: The Island Press.

LE MASTERS, E.E. (1957) Parenthood as crisis. *Marriage and Family Living* 19:352-55.

MARCIA, J.E. (1966) Development and validation of ego – Identity status. *Journal of personality and social psychology* 3:551-58.

MARCIA, J.E. and FRIEDMAN, M.L. (1970) Ego-identity status in college women. *Journal of Personality* 2:249-63.

NASH, F.W. (1973) Maternal Education and Attitudes - 100 first maternities. *Health and Social Service Journal* 83:2363-364.

PINES, D. (1972) Pregnancy and Motherhood: Interaction between fantasy and reality. *British Journal of Medical Psychology* 45: 333-48.

PITT, B. (1968) A typical depression following childbirth. *British Journal of Psychiatry* 114:1325-335.

PLESHETTE, N., ASCH, S.S., and CHEESE, J. (1956) A study of anxieties during pregnancy, labour, the early and late puerperium. *Bulletin of the New York Academy of Medicine* 32:436-55.

RACAMIER, P.C. (1961) La Mère et L'enfant dans les Psychoses du postpartum. *Evolution Psychiatrique* 10:525-76.

RAIMY, V.C. (1948) Self-reference in counselling interviews. *Journal of Consulting psychology* 12:153-63.

RHEINGOLD, J. (1964) *The Fear of Being a Woman.* New York: Grune and Stratton.

ROGERS, C. (1961) *On becoming a person.* Boston: Houghton Mifflin.

ROSSI, A. (1968) Transition to Parenthood. *Journal of Marriage and the Family* 30:26-39.

RUTTER, M. (1976) Research report. Isle of Wight Studies, 1964-74. *Psychological Medicine* 6:313-32.

SHAINESS, N. (1963) The Structure of the Mothering Encounter. *Journal of Nervous and Mental Diseases* 136:146-61.

SNYGG, D.S. and COMBS, A.W. (1949) *Individual behaviour: A new frame of reference for psychology.* New York: Harper.

THOMPSON, L.G. (1942) Attitudes of primiparae as observed in a prenatal clinic. *Mental Hygiene* 26:243-56.

WYLIE, R. (1974) *The Self Concept* (vol. 1). Lincoln, Nebraska: University of Nebraska Press.

101

Perceived costs of combining career and family roles: the influence of early family history on adult role decisions

JANET S. BERSON

Introduction

Recent work in the development of sex roles has examined the influence of maternal models on personality and career decisions (Almquist and Angrist 1971; Hoffman 1974) and on conceptions of appropriate sex-defined behaviours (Hartley 1960; 1961; Lipman-Blumen 1972; Altman 1975). Changes in career options and perceived alternatives for women who are currently making career decisions have often focussed on urging women to enter fields that are not traditionally feminine (e.g. medicine, law, and natural science rather than school teaching, nursing, and clerical work) and to plan careers defining their lives more broadly than solely in terms of mother and wife. More women seem to be trying to expand role definitions, trying to combine family and career, not choose between them.

While previous research has considered career goals primarily in terms of a stated choice (e.g. Almquist and Angrist 1971; Hoffman 1974), there has been little study of the trade-offs the young woman may think this choice involves. She may feel that combining career and motherhood is desirable, but at the same time feel that the absence of a mother when children are young deprives them of important parenting. Research examining the effects of working mothers on delinquency, school achievement, and general adjustment (Burchinal 1963; Nye 1963; Roy 1963; Hoffman 1963; 1974; Hoffman and Nye 1975) does not provide information on what aspects of the parenting role may be relevant to obtained differences between mothers who are employed in the labour market and those who are full-time housewives.

There are two aspects of the present study. In the first, perceived costs of combining roles are assessed and evaluated in the light of the employment history of the subjects' mothers. The subjects in this part of the study are single and married women. In the second part (Couples Data), differences in attitudes of husbands and wives are considered.

Perceived costs of combining roles

For all subjects, perceived cost and conflict are assessed by a test of subjective expected utility (Mausner and Leotta 1974). Various aspects of family history data were obtained through a questionnaire. Our hypotheses dealt with what issues would be most important to the subjects and with the perceived costs of having a family while working outside the home. Some of these were expected to be different for single and married subjects both because once one is in a situation, one may view it differently, and because viewing things differently may help one to choose that situation.

Our predictions dealt with four major areas:

1 quality of parenting care
2 importance of presenting a traditional female role
3 autonomy and personal development
4 threats to the marital relationship.

1 *Quality of parenting care*. No difference was predicted in values placed on aspects of child care. All subjects were

expected to rank quality child care as highly important. Married subjects were expected to see a career as involving a greater cost in this area than were single women. Women who chose to be housewives were expected to perceive a high cost in this area.

2 *Importance of presenting a traditional female role.* Single women were expected to be less concerned about fulfilling and presenting a traditional female role. This prediction was based partly on age and on the fact that the college subjects attended has a somewhat feminist orientation. We expected these women to show a more liberal view for expanding roles for women.

3 *Autonomy and personal development.* Single women were expected to be more concerned with their own needs for autonomy, valuing them more highly and seeing a career as helping to meet those needs more than did married women. Married women were expected to perceive a higher cost to leisure time when a career was pursued.

4 *Threats to the marital relationship.* All subjects were expected to value negatively threats to the marriage and to see a career as contributing to this.

METHOD

Subjects for the first part of the study were 184 women: 141 single women (four divorced with children, the others unmarried without children) and forty-three married women. All married women had at least one child, with a median number of two children. Most of the single women were between nineteen and twenty-two years of age (mostly twenty-one and twenty-two), while the married women were predominantly over twenty-three (mostly between twenty-three and thirty). Because of the confounding of age and marital status, some of the data from the two groups are reported separately and possible sources of obtained differences are noted.

Subjects were recruited from two main sources. Test materials were distributed to students in three undergraduate psychology classes at an American eastern state university and to members of a church-related discussion group in the same community. Two hundred and two questionnaires were distributed. This was the base sample for part one of the study. In the second part of the study, women in the discussion group and their husbands and both husbands and wives from a non-denominational discussion group served as subjects. The return rate was high, 94 per cent for women, 88 per cent for men. A few of the questionnaires had incomplete data.

All subjects were given the Subjective Expected Utility Scale (SEU) for pursuing a career while the mother of young children and a demographic questionnaire. Subjects were instructed to take the SEU first and were allowed to complete the forms at home, being instructed to do so without discussing their responses first. Participation was voluntary and all data were coded numerically to assure anonymity.

Figure 6(1) Sample Subjective Expected Utility (*SEU*) item (From Mausner and Leotta 1975)

How much do you care if you feel independent?

_5	_4	_3	_2	_1	0	+ 1	+ 2	+ 3	+ 4	+ 5

DON'T want it to happen   Don't care   DO want it to happen

If you DID pursue a career outside of your home, what are the chances that you would feel independent?

0	10	20	30	40	50	60	70	80	90	100

Chances in 100 that it would happen

If you DID NOT pursue a career outside of your home, what are the chances that you would feel independent?

0	10	20	30	40	50	60	70	80	90	100

Chances in 100 that it would happen

Figure 6(1) shows a sample item from the SEU. Instructions for the test were included at the beginning of the test. For each item, the subject first indicates how important an issue is to him/her and then indicates the probability that the situation will occur if the woman has a career and, then, the probability if she does not.

105

For male subjects, the form was modified to relate to values and probability regarding the wife's having a career. As can be seen from *Figure 6(1)*, an item may have a highly positive, a highly negative, or a neutral value. If the likelihood of a situation occurring is perceived to be greater when a woman has a career, the probability score will be higher on the part of the question dealing with this alternative. If the likelihood is seen to be less, the probability for 'not having a career' will be higher. If there is no difference, the scores will be about the same.

The scoring of the SEU follows from this logic. VALUE scores are those from the first part of the question, COST scores are the difference scores between the two probability estimates. The SEU score is the perceived cost weighted by the subject's own value. There are thirty-one items on the test, each having these three parts.

RESULTS

Family history variables (See *Table 6(1)*)

A comment about the married and single subjects is needed. These groups differed in several ways. The married group was older than the singles. Only ten of the single subjects were over twenty-two while only two married subjects were under twenty-three. Parents of single subjects also had slightly higher educational levels. The present data do not enable us to separate the effects of these factors.

For other subdivisions, chi-square analyses indicated that women who worked outside the home tended to have friends who did likewise ($x^2 = 28.47$, p $< .001$, df=6) and that subjects whose mother's friends worked outside the home had friends whose mothers worked similarly ($x^2 = 93.53$, p $< .001$, df=4).

More of the married subjects' mothers worked when the subjects were under fifteen and more of the older subjects' mothers worked when the subjects were over fifteen, a finding that may be affected by social class. Approximately the same percentage had mothers who did not work (19 per cent for singles, 23 per cent for marrieds).

Among the subjects' mothers, 58 per cent (n=107) were in traditional female occupations, 29 per cent (n=54) were housewives, 5 per cent (n=10) were in traditional occupations to non-traditional levels, and 4 per cent (n=8) were in non-traditional occupations. A chi-square for mother's occupation and daughter's stated career goal was not significant.

A higher proportion of single women had non-traditional career goals than did married women (35 per cent to 9 per cent) but the groups were even for traditional careers even to non-traditional levels (twenty-three and 3 per cent to twenty-six and 5 per cent). Career goals here refers to occupational choices including working inside or outside the home. The former includes being a full-time housewife and mother. Married women indicated being a housewife as their 'career' goal more often than did single women (39 per cent to 9 per cent). Over all groups single women answered this question more often than did married women (6 per cent to 39 per cent).

Value, cost, and subjective expected utility scores

Mean scores for value and for cost were obtained for each item. The range of scores indicates that the items measure different aspects of the effects of role combination.

To make the data more manageable, a rotated orthogonal factor analysis was carried out (DATA-TEXT, Armor, and Couch 1972). Separate factor analyses were made for VALUE scores, COST scores and SEU scores. Because the obtained factors were in terms of z-scores, actual relative scores were calculated to enable a comparison of scores across factors (i.e. were scores higher for *autonomy* than for *traditional* roles?) as well as across subgroups (i.e. did married and single subjects rate autonomy needs differently?). Items correlating at .40 or greater were included in factor scores. There were six factors for each of the three sets of scores. Means and standard deviations for factors were calculated. *Table 6(2)* shows the factors for the three sets of scores.

The sample was subdivided on the basis of different aspects of personal history and mean factor scores for Value, Cost, and SEU were calculated for each group. (See *Table 6(1)* for the number of subjects in each subgrouping.)

The most highly valued items were those involving personal independence and feelings of worth and those involving care of children. The most negatively valued items dealt with having outside interests threaten the marriage and having others care for children.

Items for which there was the greatest perceived gain with a

Table 6(1) *Distribution of subjects based on family history variables*

	Single	Married	Total
Number of subjects	141	43	184
Mother's working status: age of subject			
under 15 only	18	11	29
over 15 only	40	6	46
both under and over 15	59	15	74
did not work	26	10	35
Mother's friends' work history:			
yes	40	5	45
some	43	13	56
no	39	16	55
Friends' mother's work history:			
yes	35	3	39
some	36	18	57
no	49	13	63
Career goal:			
non-traditional area	49	4	53
traditional area	32	11	43
traditional area at non-traditional level	8	2	10
housewife/marriage	13	13	26
none stated	39	1	40

career were primarily autonomy needs and those involving the husband more in household responsibilities and child care. Those items showing the greatest perceived loss with a career were those dealing with leisure time and with the child's experiencing traditional parental roles. Items relating to children feeling loved, having consistent discipline, and the wife's being relaxed when her husband returns from work showed minimal cost (this last may be unlikely in either condition!).

An analysis of variance revealed significant differences between subgroups. For groups based on marital status and age, there was a difference in the importance of presenting a traditional role but not for any other VALUE score. Over all groups, there were few differences in VALUE scores. Based on marital status, difference in COST is seen in autonomy and leisure needs and in an increased need for spouse involvement. Grouping by age changes these results only in the area of autonomy.

A similar pattern is found for women whose mothers worked with the largest differences (using a Scheffé test for anova results) between groups whose mothers worked when the children were under fifteen and those whose mothers did not work. When mother's friends worked, the pattern was also similar with an increased stress on parenting issues.

When we consider the subject's own career goal, differences also emerge only in COST and SEU scores. Here, for the first time, they dealt with child-rearing variables. Because of the nature of this subdivision, we have accentuated any perceived differences between those women who choose to be housewives and those who may choose careers outside the home. No significant differences were found based on whether subjects' friends' mothers worked.

Our prediction regarding child care was supported. Subjects did not differ significantly in their view about the value and importance of child care. Having a career outside the home was not seen as detrimental to child care by four of the five comparison groups. On average women who rated having a career as negatively affecting child care were those who were currently staying or who planned to stay at home full-time when children were young. The findings here may reflect justification for the choices they had made.

The SEU factor involving child care that does seem to differentiate between subgroups includes several items that do not uniformly deal with child care but also refer to observing a child's development and to social aspects of parenting.

The prediction about the need to fulfil a traditional female role being more important for married and for older subjects was supported. Again, the confounding of the two variables makes the meaning of this unclear.

While we had predicted a difference in the way single and married women viewed autonomy and personal development, differences were found only in COST and SEU scores. These women may not value these needs differently but may see a career as affecting them differently. Perhaps our married subjects

Table 6(2) *Factor scores based on SEU test.*

Value factors

Autonomy
Traditional role: caretaking
Parenting role: available to children
Leisure for children
Homemaking skills
Negative effects on marriage

Cost factors

Autonomy
Own leisure needs
Father's role
Parenting contact and negative effects on marriage
Modelling of traditional role
Performing traditional female role (also having children and
    husband help at home)

Subjective expected utility factors

Autonomy
Performing traditional female role
Father's role
Social functions in parenting
Homemaking role
Maternal role: responsiveness to child's needs

---

have found other means of attaining these needs. We did not get any information about their hobbies, volunteer or organizational work history, or related issues.

The fourth area, threats to the marriage, did not differ between the groups. This may reflect the lack of sensitivity in our measure or actual absence of differences. The subjects did indicate the increased importance of the father's assistance in terms of helping with household responsibilities when the mother worked outside the home. The need for moral support was not assessed although one might hypothesize that it would also be relevant.

Couples data

A brief comment on the couples' data will be made at this point. Items more highly rated by women than by their husbands primarily included autonomy needs. Those items that men viewed more negatively involved having housework done. Women saw greater costs in independence and in the need to have others care for their children, while men viewed the need for their greater involvement in household tasks as the greatest cost.

This may reflect a difference between these men and women in the way they viewed the women's needs for autonomy and in the way these are affected by working outside the home. Each sex seemed to respond most strongly to issues that affected their own roles and responsibilities. Total SEU scores were higher for women than for men, indicating that they saw greater gains in their having a career outside the home than their husbands saw for them. The small sample size and the fact that we have not completed the statistical analyses for this sample makes the above findings only suggestive of differences in attitudes. In general, there was considerable agreement within a couple on the items.

Summary and further discussion

The primary findings reported here suggest that the perceived gain of combining a career and family lies mainly in the area of increased autonomy and that the perceived cost is in presenting a traditional female role. Other studies reveal similar findings (Nevill and Damico 1974) through other means of assessment. The loss in terms of leisure time and, furthermore, the need for co-operation from one's spouse are confirmed through discussions with women who are trying to combine the two roles. One's attitudes about the costs involved thus are affected by having been in the situation, either through having had a working mother or having children of one's own. Both of these factors make the experience of issues involved in parenting while working more realistic. Once a woman has been a parent and has experienced the responsibilities involved, she may greatly alter

111

her view of how working would affect her role as a mother. In making plans for one's life before actually becoming a parent, one relies in part on personal experiences. One experience we have not discussed is that of the woman whose mother did not work and who was dissatisfied with her role as housewife.

The data for couples will be more fully examined in the next phase of the research. We intend to consider other populations as well, including, it is hoped, women who are actively involved in role combination. It will be important to consider how the actual and anticipated reactions of men affect the decisions a woman makes. We are also regrouping the factors on a rational rather than an empirical basis; derived in this way they may be more homogeneous.

A wide range of factors influence role choices. By better understanding the conflict and considering the reality of our options, making choices can become less conflict-laden and we may know what resources we need to help facilitate a wider variety of situations for ourselves and for our children.

References

ALMQUIST, E.M. and ANGRIST, S.S. (1971) Role model influences on college women's career aspirations. *Merrill Palmer Quarterly* **17**:263-79.

ALTMAN, S. (1975) Women's career plans and maternal employment. *Dissertation Abstracts International*.

ARMOR D.J. and COUCH, A.S. (1972) *DATA-TEXT Primer*. Glencoe: Free Press.

BURCHINAL, L.G. (1963) Personality characteristics of children. In, F.I. Nye and L.W. Hoffman (eds), *The Employed Mother in America*. Chicago: Rand McNally.

DOUVAN, E. (1963) Employment and the adolescent. In, F.I. Nye and L.W. Hoffman (eds), *The Employed Mother in America*. Chicago: Rand McNally.

FRANKEL, P.M. (1974) Sex-role attitudes and the development of achievement motivation need in women. *Journal of College Student Personnel* **15**(2):114-19.

HARTLEY, R.E. (1960) Children's concepts of male and female roles. *Merrill Palmer Quarterly* **6**:83-91.

——(1961) What aspects of child behaviour should be studied in relation to maternal employment? In, A.E. Seigel (ed.), *Research Issues Related to the Effects of Maternal Employment on Children*. University Park, Pennsylvania: Social Science Research Center.

HOFFMAN, L.W. (1963) Effects on children: Summary and discussion. In, F.I. Nye and L.W. Hoffman (eds), *The Employed Mother in America*. Chicago: Rand McNally.

—— (1974) Effects of maternal employment on the child: A review of the research. *Developmental Psychology* 10(2):204-28.

HOFFMAN, L.W. and NYE, F.I. (1975) *Working Mothers*. San Francisco: Jossey-Bass.

LIPMAN-BLUMEN, J. (1972) How ideology shapes women's lives. *Scientific American* 226 (1): 34–42.

MAUSNER, B. and LEOTTA, S. (1974) Expected utility differences in women returning vs. those not returning to college (unpublished manuscript).

NEVILL, D. and DAMICO, S. (1974) Development of a role conflict questionnaire for women. *Journal of Consulting and Clinical Psychology* 42(5):743.

NEMEROWICZ, G. (1978) Sex roles and work roles: Children's perspectives. Rutgers University (unpublished doctoral dissertation).

NYE, F.I. (1963) The adjustment of adolescent children. In, F.I. Nye and L.W. Hoffman (eds) *The Employed Mother In America*. Chicago: Rand McNally.

ROY, P. (1963) Adolescent roles: rural-urban differentials. In, F.I. Nye and L.W. Hoffman (eds) *The Employed Mother in America*. Chicago: Rand McNally.

YARROWM, M.R., SCOTT, P., DELEEUW, L., and HENIG, G.C. (1962) Childrearing in families of working and non-working mothers. *Sociometry* 25:122-40.

PART THREE

Success and failure

SEVEN

Sex differences in explanations of success and failure

NICOLE VIAENE

The literature concerning sex differences in causal attributions for success and failure can be summarized as follows: males tend to attribute their success more to ability than females, whereas females show more luck attributions for both success and failure than males. Some studies also suggest that more girls than boys attribute their failure to lack of ability. (For a more detailed review, see Frieze 1975.) Deaux and Farris (1977) have recently theorized that the overall pattern of sex differences in causal attributions appears clearest if a general expectancy model is considered. In this model, performance consistent with expectations is attributed to a stable internal factor (ability) while performance inconsistent with expectations is attributed to one or more temporary factors (luck, effort). As Deaux and Farris reasoned, as the expectancies of women and men differ, so attribution patterns will differ as well. Men, having more positive expectations than women, will be more likely to explain their success in terms of their own ability, while women who succeed despite their own expectations will attribute their success to some temporary factor such as luck. Conversely, because women have lower expectations, a failure is less likely to disconfirm their predictions and the stable explanation of lack of ability is more readily invoked. Men, in contrast, find failure unexpected and are more prone to use an unstable reason for its occurrence. Valle and Frieze (1976) developed a similar model and related the types of causal attribution with future expectations of success.

An explanation of sex differences in causal attributions as a function of sex differences in expectancy of success seems to be promising and merits further investigation on two counts. First, because the literature has indicated large sex differences in initial expectation of success (for a review see Frieze 1975; Maccoby and Jacklin 1975; Lenney 1977). Second, the expectancy model itself has received wide empirical support for both other attributions (Feather and Simon 1971a; Frieze and Weiner 1971) and self-attributions (Feather 1969; Feather and Simon 1971a; 1971b; Simon and Feather 1973): the greater the difference between an outcome (whether success or failure) and previous expectations the greater the tendency to attribute the outcome to luck (and sometimes also to effort); the less the difference between an outcome and previous expectations the greater the tendency to attribute the outcome to ability (and sometimes also to task attributes).

It is not expected that the general expectancy model can explain all sex differences in causal attributions mentioned in the literature. Some studies (Bar-Tal and Frieze 1977; Feather 1969) that have been cited by Deaux and Farris (1977) as empirical evidence consistent with the general expectancy interpretation, only partially support their views, especially those studies in which females use more luck attributions for both success *and* failure, the latter result being inconsistent with the general expectancy interpretation. Therefore, we have to consider other variables and processes that can explain this general external orientation of females.

Frieze *et al.* (in press) have suggested that this pattern of luck attributions among females implies that, at least within traditionally masculine areas, women take less responsibility for and feel less pride in their successes and feel less shame about their failures.

118

In such situations women are less likely to try to achieve success and would experience relatively little affect in relation to their achievement. In addition, such an indifference to achievement may be more prevalent among subjects with a feminine self-concept. Hence, we would expect a positive relationship between femininity and luck attributions for both success and failure. However, there is also some evidence that females who manifest achievement efforts in areas that are usually considered masculine do not necessarily have a low identification with the feminine role, but they do have a relatively high masculine role identification (Stein and Bailey 1973). That is, they may be categorized as androgynous individuals (Bem 1974), being both masculine and feminine in their self-concept, both assertive and yielding, both instrumental and expressive, depending on the situational appropriateness of these various behaviours.

In her laboratory studies, Bem provides empirical evidence that androgynous individuals not only perform cross-sex behaviour with little reluctance or discomfort (Bem and Lenney 1976) but display both 'masculine' independence when under pressure to conform as well as 'feminine' nurturance when given the opportunity to interact with both a baby kitten (Bem 1975) and a human infant or to listen to a lonely student (Bem et al. 1976).

The wider study of which this paper is only a part aims to evaluate further the utility and construct validity of the androgyny concept and to examine the separate influence of femininity and masculinity on causal attributions of success and failure. Consistent with Bem's assertions, it will be hypothesized that androgynous individuals will engage in the most appropriate pattern of reaction, at least as much as male subjects in a sex-appropriate achievement situation.

It is contended that the most appropriate cognitions in this context are those that serve to maintain a high self-esteem. Weiner et al. (1972) and Weiner (1974) have shown that more pride or satisfaction is reported by people who attribute their successes internally than if the attribution is made to an external cause. These same studies have found that internally attributed failures lead to more shame or dissatisfaction after failure.

Therefore it may be hypothesized that androgynous and masculine subjects are more likely to attribute their successes and less likely to attribute their failures to internal causes (ability) than feminine subjects. There arises a problem when one tries to predict the degree of and reasons for luck attributions after failure: while masculine and androgynous individuals are expected to be external in order to defend their high achievement-related self-esteem, feminine subjects might give luck attributions for failure because they may be uninterested in achievement and because some lack of power of the female to control her own destiny is part of the cultural stereotype of femininity (Maccoby and Jacklin 1975).

A more direct test of this latter assumption would be to examine the relationship between external locus of control (I-E construct of Rotter (1966)) of males and females and their causal attributions. Frieze *et al.* (in press) have also suggested that a greater external locus of control in females might be responsible for their greater luck attributions for both success and failure.

Method

SUBJECTS AND GENERAL PROCEDURE

Study 1

The subjects were 142 students (eighty male, sixty-two female) from the last three years of a co-educational Catholic high school in a small city in the country. Subjects were fifteen to eighteen years old. They were tested (by the author) in three form groups in regular school hours. Code numbers were used to preserve anonymity. The data for the first study were gathered in May 1976. In the first study the Bem Sex Role Inventory (BSRI) was administered with the instruction to indicate how well each of the sixty masculine, feminine, and neutral personality characteristics described themselves (on seven-point scales), followed by an assessment of the expectancy of success, performance, and causal attributions on an anagrams task. Finally there was a re-administration of the BSRI: one half of the subjects were instructed to rate the social desirability of the items for a boy in our society, with the other half rating the social desirability for a girl in our society.

Study 2

The second study was designed to test the generality of the findings of the first study and to evaluate the value of the locus of control construct in explaining sex differences in causal attributions. The subjects were 218 students (114 male, 103 female) from the last three years of three co-educational Catholic high schools located in three different small cities. Subjects were fifteen to eighteen years old. They were tested by one or two female experimenters (the author and/or M. Van Dijck) in November 1976. For the second study, the sequence of the test administration was as follows:

1 Locus of control questionnaire: the 'Internal versus External' control scale of Andriessen (1972), an adapted questionnaire of the locus of control scale of Rotter (1966), was used as a measure of locus of control.
2 BSRI scale, to assess individual sex-typing.
3 Anagrams task, with the measurement of expectancy of success, performance, and causal attributions.

ADMINISTRATION OF THE PERFORMANCE TASK (ANAGRAMS TEST)

In both studies, test outcome (success or failure) was controlled by manipulation of item difficulty. In each group the two sets of anagrams were randomly distributed in equal numbers among subjects. Subjects in the failure conditions received six insoluble items, two soluble but difficult anagrams, and two easy anagrams. The easy list consisted of two insoluble items, two soluble but rather difficult anagrams, and six easy items. There were eight different randomly chosen sequences and each anagram was printed on a separate page of a test booklet. Unlike other researchers, we allowed subjects five minutes to work at ten anagrams and imposed only one time limit (instead of ten time limits of thirty seconds). This was done because testing occurred in rather large groups and to minimize suspicion from the subjects.

The anagrams task was introduced as follows:

'Now you will get a task that takes ten minutes to solve. On each page of a test booklet you will find six letters. When you rearrange the sequence of some of the letters, you will find a meaningful Dutch word of six letters. The words you have to search for can be nouns or verbs (no proper names or adjectives). In all you will have ten such problems (anagrams) to solve. Almost nobody has the same sequence, so it doesn't help to look at your neighbour's. Don't spend too much time at one anagram when you can't solve it immediately. First try to solve those you find rather quickly and then look again at those you didn't find immediately. You may write down preliminary solutions.

Previous investigations in other schools have shown the mean number of correct solutions to be somewhere between four or five. However there are great individual differences. Those who have all the problems correct are very rare, so are those who haven't any anagram correct. To succeed you must have at least five correct solutions. If you have only four or less problems correct then you have failed. Now look into the envelope, take the booklet and put it in front of you. Before opening the booklet, read the two questions on the first page and answer them.'

These two questions measured the expectancy of success. Question 1 asked the subjects how many anagrams they expected to solve correctly (this variable will be called 'expa'). The second question asked the subjects to indicate how confident they were they could pass the test (this variable will be called 'confid').

After completing the task, subjects were asked to count up the number of anagrams they had solved in the time allowed. They were cautioned not to change any answers and were asked to write down their total score on the first page of the booklet and to indicate if they succeeded or failed.

POST-PERFORMANCE QUESTIONNAIRE

In both studies subjects who passed the test were asked to answer Part 1 of a post-performance questionnaire. Subjects who failed the test were asked to answer Part 2 of the questionnaire. The instructions of the questionnaire were the same as those used by Feather (1971a). Subjects assigned responsibility for test outcome by rating the degree to which the outcome was attributable to ability (or lack of ability), effort (or lack of effort), task difficulty (easy or hard), and luck (good or bad). Subjects put crosses on four seven-point scales. For the success group these were labelled 'easy task', 'tried hard', 'good luck', and 'skill and ability', and each scale had the statement 'not a cause' at one extreme, the statement 'very much a cause' at the other extreme. They were scored one to seven in the direction of increasing causality. For the failure group the scales were labelled 'difficult task', 'did not try hard', 'bad luck', and 'lack of skill and ability', with the same statements at the extremes as in the success group. They were also scored one to seven in the direction of increasing causality.

Subjects also indicated on seven-point scales how satisfied they were with their score and how much they would enjoy taking a similar anagrams test.

Form of analysis and presentation

COMPARISONS BETWEEN SEXES ON CASUAL ATTRIBUTIONS

Separately for Study 1 and Study 2

Several multiple regression analyses (Kerlinger and Pedhazur 1973) were carried out in which each type of causal attribution functioned as a dependent variable. In each case, the following 'predictor' variables were successively entered into the regression equation: test outcome, sex, and a product variable obtained through multiplication of sex by test outcome. The latter term is expected to be significant from the viewpoint of the expectancy interpretation.

The two studies combined

Further multiple regression analyses were conducted with respect to each outcome separately, that is, for subjects who succeeded and for subjects who failed the anagrams test, with sex, schools (all four schools were included in the analyses), and the product term of school and sex as independent variables (to examine the possibility of a different pattern of sex differences across the schools).

The relationship between CA and *expectancy of success* was assessed for Study 1 and Study 2 and is reported later under 'Analysis of sex differences in CA in relation to the general expectancy model'.

The relationship between CA and *psychological sex-typing* was assessed separately for boys and girls who succeeded or failed in each of the four schools.

The relationship between CA and *locus of control* was assessed only for subjects of Schools 2, 3, and 4 (i.e. Study 2).

Relationships were assessed by computing Pearson product-moment correlations within each sex group. In some cases, analyses of covariance could be conducted to determine whether a sex difference in CA could be accounted for by a sex difference in other 'predictor' variables.

Results

CHECK ON THE MANIPULATION OF TEST OUTCOME

The manipulation of test outcome was successful in each school: there was a highly significant difference in mean number of correct solutions between subjects who failed and those who succeeded in each of the four schools. In the success condition both sexes performed equally well; there was, however, in the failure condition a trend for boys to perform better than girls (in some schools only).

COMPARISONS BETWEEN BOYS AND GIRLS ON CAUSAL ATTRIBUTIONS

Study 1

The effect of sex was significant for three of the four causal attributions: girls gave more luck ($F=5.19$, $df=1/139$, $p<.05$) and fewer ability attributions ($F=6.61$, $df=1/139$, $p<.05$) than boys. Girls also tended to give fewer effort attributions than boys ($F=3.83$, $df=1/139$, $p<.10$). However, the interaction term of sex and test outcome was *not* significant: there occurred no reversal of sex differences in luck and ability attributions as a function of test outcome.

Within the *success* condition, two of the four causal attributions showed significant sex differences : girls attributed their success more to good luck and less to ability than boys (p $<$ .02 resp. p $<$ .05, one-tailed t-test). Within the *failure* group, boys attributed their failure more than girls to difficulty of the task and to lack of ability (p $<$ .10 resp. p. $<$ .05, t-tailed two-test), the latter result being in strong contradiction with the hypothesis.

Study 2

The interaction of sex and test outcome proved to be significant for ability attributions (F=6.47, dfl=/214, p $<$ .05). Girls attributed their *failure* more to lack of ability than boys ($\overline{X}$ girls=3.74 to $\overline{X}$ boys=2.95, p $<$ .01), while there was a non-significant trend for boys to explain their successes more in terms of ability ($\overline{X}$ boys=4.56 to $\overline{X}$ girls=4.33). There was no parallel interaction on luck attributions : on the contrary, consistent with the first study, girls tended to attribute their outcomes more to luck factors (F=2.90, df=1/215, p $<$ .10). Girls attributed their *success* significantly more to good luck than boys ($\overline{X}$ girls = 4.62 to $\overline{X}$ boys = 4.17, p $<$ .10); the sex difference for luck explanations in the failure condition was in the same direction, but did not reach significance ($\overline{X}$ girls = 4.45 to $\overline{X}$ boys = 4.16).

The two studies combined

Separate analyses for success and failure groups across the four schools revealed a significant interaction effect of school and sex on lack of ability attributions (F=11.11, df=3/172, p $<$ .01) (see *Table 7(1)*). The significant interaction of school and sex is reflected in the pattern of opposite sex differences across schools: in Schools 1 and 2, boys attribute their failure more to lack of ability (p $<$ .01 in School 1) than girls. In the other two schools, girls show significantly more lack of ability attributions than boys (p $<$ .01), a result that is consistent with both the expectancy model and the previous literature.

125

Table 7(1) *Means and standard deviations of causal attributions for boys and girls who failed or succeeded in each of the four schools.*

| | Success (n = 179) | | | | | | Failure (n = 180) | | | | | |
| | Boys | | | Girls | | | Boys | | | Girls | | |
	M	SD	n	M	SD	n	M	SD	n	M	SD	n
School 1 (Diksmuide)			40			33			40			29
Task	3.90	1.39		4.09	1.58		4.00	1.52		3.34	1.54	
Effort	4.60	1.26		4.21	1.25		3.60	1.70		3.03	1.42	
Luck	3.28	1.53		4.12	1.55		3.60	1.82		4.07	1.96	
Ability	4.40	1.24		3.91	1.21		3.48	1.47		2.86	0.99	
School 2 (Lokeren)			20			20			23			17
Task	3.91	1.61		4.20	1.10		4.26	1.36		3.53	1.38	
Effort	4.24	1.64		4.95	1.15		3.04	1.69		3.41	1.84	
Luck	4.29	1.62		4.40	1.19		4.00	1.71		5.00	1.4	
Ability	4.43	1.69		4.50	1.00		3.52	1.47		2.82	1.33	
School 3 (Haacht)			30			13			26			23
Task	3.97	1.45		4.38	1.04		3.96	1.80		4.04	1.22	
Effort	4.63	1.35		5.08	1.12		3.31	1.85		3.43	1.70	
Luck	4.10	1.79		5.31	1.11		4.35	1.57		4.83	1.47	
Ability	4.53	1.33		4.23	1.59		2.62	1.27		3.96	1.63	
School 4 (Leuven)			8			15			7			15
Task	5.12	1.73		4.20	1.21		3.14	1.95		4.27	1.71	
Effort	4.12	2.03		4.33	1.05		3.43	1.90		3.00	1.60	
Luck	4.12	2.23		4.33	1.76		4.00	1.73		3.27	1.49	
Ability	5.00	1.51		4.20	1.57		2.29	1.11		4.47	1.69	

Analysis of sex differences in causal attributions in relation to the general expectancy model

In the *first* study, sex differences in causal attributions are not consistent with the general expectancy model. Two reasons are suggested for the failure to obtain the hypothetical interaction of sex and test outcome:

1 There should be no sex differences in expectancy of success. However, the results strongly indicate that boys expect to solve significantly more anagrams ($F=10.72$, $df=1/140$, $p < .01$) and are significantly more confident of success than girls ($F=20.29$, $df=1/140$, $p < .01$).

2 A second possible reason could be a failure to verify the expectancy model itself. However, the expectancy model received wide empirical support: there is a significant interaction of test outcome and initial confidence for both luck ($F=4.46$, $df=1/138$, $p < .05$) and ability attributions ($F=8.22$, $df=1/138$, $p < .01$). Thus, unexpected outcomes are more attributed to luck and expected outcomes more to ability.

In the *second* study, however, sex differences in ability attributions are consistent with the general expectancy interpretation. In order to determine whether this sex difference can be accounted for by sex differences in expectancy of success, an analysis of covariance was conducted, in which expectancy of success was held (statistically) constant. If sex differences in ability attributions disappear after removing sex differences in expectancy, we have evidence that sex differences in ability attributions are mediated by sex differences in expectancy. If they do not disappear, we have no evidence that sex differences in expectancy are the crucial factor in determining sex differences in ability attributions. Results from this analysis of covariance show that sex differences in ability attributions continue to exist (F value for the interaction of sex and test outcome $= 6.66$, $df=1/213$, $p < .01$ after controlling for expa; $F=6.80$, $df=1/213$, $p < .01$, after controlling for confid.). Thus, although in this second study all the conditions of the general expectancy model were verified – that is, there were highly significant sex differences in expectancy of success (F=13.76, df=1/214, p $<$.01 for expa; F=20.93, df=1/214, p $<$.01 for confid.), the expectancy model did receive wide empirical support (there was a significant interaction of expectancy of success and test outcome on both luck and ability attribution (both p $<$.01)), and there was a significant interaction of sex and test outcome on ability attributions – although all these requirements were met, we have *no* evidence that these sex differences in ability attributions were *due* to sex differences in expectancy of success.

Analysis of causal attributions of boys and girls in relation to psychological sex-typing

The Bem Sex Role Inventory (BSRI) provides separate femininity and masculinity scale scores and uses their t-ratio difference as a measure of psychological androgyny. Positive androgyny scores indicate a generally more feminine orientation, negative scores a more masculine one, and scores near zero an androgynous orientation. We investigated whether masculine and androgynous individuals would both give the same appropriate causal attributions as opposed to feminine subjects. We examined whether the relationship between androgyny score and causal attributions deviated significantly from linearity. However, in most instances, such a relation was not obtained. There were two exceptions, however: androgynous individuals in Study 1 gave as many effort attributions as masculine individuals after success, both scoring significantly higher than feminine subjects. Also, androgynous subjects of both sexes in School 3 tended to attribute their failure less to lack of ability than either masculine or feminine subjects.

Table 7(2) gives the (linear) relationships between sex-typing measures and social desirability scores on the one hand and causal attributions on the other hand, separately for boys and girls (in each school).

The hypothesis that masculinity would be positively associated with an explanation of success in terms of ability received empirical support in three of the four female groups and in one of the male groups. In these female subgroups, there was also a positive relationship between 'positive self-presentation' and ability attributions. The partial correlation coefficient between

128

masculinity and ability attributions after controlling for positive self-presentation was significant for females in School 1 (.28) and School 2 (.49), while it diminished to a non-significant level for the females in School 3 (.25).

The hypothesis that femininity would be negatively associated with ability attributions received only weak support : the correlation reached significance (at the 1 per cent level) in one subgroup, boys at School 3, while it was also significant for boys in School 1, after controlling for positive self-presentation (−.27).

Contrary to prediction, masculine boys who *failed* attributed their failure more to lack of ability than low masculine boys in School 1. Such a positive correlation was also found for boys in School 2, which was significant after controlling for positive self-presentation (.32). In the other subgroups, there was no relation between masculinity and lack of ability attributions. Femininity, on the other hand, tended to be associated with attributions of lack of ability in three of the four female groups and in two of the four male groups.

It is worth noting that in each of the eight subsamples there was a positive relationship between 'negative self-presentation' and lack of ability attributions, which reached significance in six of the eight subgroups. The hypothesis that both masculinity and femininity would be positively associated with luck attributions after failure received support in only one subgroup (girls in School 1). For the girls and boys of Schools 2 and 3, there emerged a complex pattern of relationships between sex-typing and luck attributions for failure. As predicted, masculinity correlated positively with luck attributions, but only for girls. Contrary to prediction, masculinity correlated negatively with luck for boys. As predicted, femininity correlated positively with luck attributions, but only for boys. Contrary to prediction, femininity correlated negatively with luck attributions for girls (in both groups after controlling for positive and negative self-presentation). The same finding is reflected in the pattern of relationships between androgyny score and luck attributions : the more feminine a boy, the more he explains his failure by luck; the more feminine a girl, the less she explains her failure by luck. Or, stated in still another way : *traditionally sex-typed individuals* of *both sexes* (masculine males and feminine females) give *less luck* attributions for failure, while *opposite sex-typed individuals* (feminine males and masculine females) give *more luck* attributions after failure.

Table 7(2) Pearson correlations between causal attributions and various BSRI scales

		Androgyny		Masculinity		Femininity		Positive self-presentation		Negative self-presentation	
		S	F	S	F	S	F	S	F	S	F
Girls of School 1											
n of s = 33	Task	.01	.06	−.24	−.10	−.20	−.03	−.31**	.09	.19	−.24
n off = 29	Effort	−.26	−.20	−.04	.04	−.32*	−.33*	−.09	−.40**	.16	.33**
	Luck	−.10	−.04	−.08	.35*	−.07	.40**	−.15	.43†	.26	.23
	Ability	−.07	−.01	.37**	.09	.22	.15	.32**	.18	−.18	.32**
Girls of School 2											
n of s = 20	Task	−.21	.09	.15	−.14	.05	.13	−.22	.04	.06	−.20
n off = 17	Effort	.01	.14	−.11	−.06	−.11	−.09	.01	−.38*	−.04	−.26
	Luck	.05	−.64†	−.20	.35*	−.19	−.29	−.50†	.40*	−.05	.33
	Ability	−.47**	.15	.54†	.03	−.24	.29	.40**	.07	.03	.16
Girls of School 3											
n of s = 13	Task	.26	−.11	.13	.23	.53**	.14	.27	.00	−.07	.08
n off = 23	Effort	.41*	.15	−.40*	.00	−.26	.26	−.09	.27*	−.38*	−.02
	Luck	.06	−.18	.14	.45†	.40*	.29*	.25	.43**	−.42*	−.22
	Ability	−.37	.11	.46*	.11	−.04	.36**	.62†	.15	.28	.31*
Girls of School 4											
n of s = 15	Task	−.36	−.23	.52**	.40*	.39*	.11	.47**	−.00	.11	.27
n off = 15	Effort	.21	.44**	−.29	−.27	.19	.63†	.00	.04	−.19	−.38*
	Luck	.38*	.00	−.16	−.01	.54**	.09	.32	.00	−.09	−.26
	Ability	−.03	.05	−.11	−.11	.02	−.21	−.41*	−.08	.67†	.38*

Boys of School 1										
n of s = 40	Task	−.15	.13	.15	−.13	−.06	−.00	−.07	−.01	.15	.04
n of f = 40	Effort	.09	−.20	.05	.05	.13	−.21	.09	−.18	.03	.19
	Luck	.01	−.07	−.01	−.08	−.03	−.23	−.04	−.09	.17	.02
	Ability	−.40†	−.23	.44†	.32**	−.20	.17	.10	.01	.02	.40†

Boys of School 2										
n of s = 20	Task	.00	−.28	.17	.14	.14	−.31*	.31*	−.07	−.12	.09
n of f = 23	Effort	−.36*	.20	.07	−.17	−.32*	.04	.00	−.15	.13	.13
	Luck	.14	.30*	.13	−.27*	.21	.22	−.12	−.21	.22	.23
	Ability	−.15	−.21	.06	.24	−.06	−.03	.06	−.01	−.18	.25

Boys of School 3										
n of s = 30	Task	.08	−.05	.02	−.07	.28*	−.04	.32**	−.23	.17	−.13
n of f = 26	Effort	−.12	−.10	−.03	.07	−.29*	−.18	.04	−.03	−.23	.18
	Luck	.37**	.32**	−.40†	−.41†	.30*	.11	−.18	−.02	.50*	−.27
	Ability	−.12	−.19	−.08	.10	−.41†	−.10	−.35**	−.10	−.18	.21

Boys of School 4										
n of s = 8	Task	−.69**	.35	.51*	−.01	−.51*	.59	.10	.32	−.66**	.60
n of f = 7	Effort	.23	.70*	−.40	−.45	−.03	.60	−.60*	.08	.01	.15
	Luck	−.12	−.03	−.06	.15	−.32	−.12	−.48	−.04	.40	−.10
	Ability	−.06	.35	−.27	.11	−.27	.79**	.12	.33	−.15	.79**

$*p < .05$ $**p < .01$ $†p < .10$

s = success
f = failure

In conclusion it would seem that degree of sex-typing as measured in this study can hardly be considered a crucial factor in explaining sex differences in causal attributions. There is only one exception: in School 1 there was no longer evidence for sex differences in lack of ability attributions after controlling for masculinity of the subjects (that is after removing sex differences in masculinity by means of an analysis of covariance).

Analysis of causal attributions of boys and girls in relation to locus of control

In the present study, internal-external locus of control will not be helpful for explaining sex differences in causal attributions, since there were no sex differences in the measure of locus of control used.

Nevertheless, it is worth noting that there were substantial positive correlations between an external locus of control and luck attributions after both success and failure, and substantial negative correlations with effort attributions after both success and failure (but not always significantly for both sexes). However, significant (negative) correlations between ability attributions and external locus of control emerged only for boys who succeeded.

If a measure of locus of control could be developed that is more sensitive to sex differences (which might be possible since it is generally assumed that females have less control over life events than men) or if an older age group were used, perhaps sex differences in luck attributions could be explained.

Discussion

CONCERNING COMPARISONS BETWEEN BOYS AND GIRLS ON CAUSAL ATTRIBUTIONS

Consistent with the literature, in both studies males tended to attribute their success more to ability than females, whereas females showed more luck attributions for both success and failure than males (although the sex difference did not always reach statistical significance). The greater lack of ability attributions in Study 2 was also consistent with the literature (see e.g. Frieze 1975). Only the results of Study 1, in which males gave more lack

132

of ability attributions than females, were at odds with previous findings. When a more detailed analysis was carried out, there was a second subgroup (School 2) in which boys tended to attribute their failure more to lack of ability than girls. We could not find any evidence of sex differences in expectancy of success, psychological androgyny, or locus of control that interacted with the schools. So we can only speculate about the characteristics of the schools or pupils that could lead to a different pattern in sex differences in CA. While the four schools resembled each other in many respects (all Catholic, rather small, co-educational schools in rather small cities), it must be said that the subjects of School 4 formed a distinct group: in addition to their normal school curriculum, they all followed a lot of music courses. The main reason for their being at that school was music. However, it was the only co-educational school in which there were more females than males. Perhaps these are the reasons why these subjects displayed causal attributions that were consistent with predictions. It could be hypothesized that in single-sex schools (which is the general rule in the Belgian Catholic school system), the differences between the sexes on causal attributions will be more consistent with predictions, females displaying a typical feminine pattern and males a typical masculine pattern.

From a theoretical point of view, boys are expected to make more lack of ability attributions for a failure on a *feminine* task than girls (since they should also have lower expectancies of success). In our current research, we have varied the sex-typing of the task and were able to support this hypothesis. Rosenfield and Stephan (1978) have also reported that males made more lack of ability attributions on a feminine task, while they made fewer lack of ability attributions on a masculine task. So the hypothesis can be advanced that subjects of Schools 1 and 2 perceived the anagrams task as a rather feminine task while pupils of the other two schools considered it a masculine task.

CONCERNING THE RELATIONSHIP OF CAUSAL ATTRIBUTIONS WITH PREDICTOR VARIABLES

It is worth noting that there was *no* evidence that sex differences in *expectancy of success* should play a crucial role in explaining sex differences in causal attributions, not even in those cases where sex differences in ability attributions were entirely consistent with a general expectancy interpretation.

The results of this study illustrate that it is not because one variable (i.e. expectancy) is associated with another (causal attributions) *within* each sex, that this same variable (expectancy) in which sex differences occur necessarily accounts for differences *between* sexes in the other variable (causal attributions).

This supposition has now been tested, and no empirical evidence has been found. These results also cast serious doubt on the effectiveness of change programmes for women, in which, according to Frieze (1975) direct attributional therapy is necessary to increase expectancies in women with low estimates of their ability. The present study suggests that the crucial variable has not yet been identified.

Two reasons are suggested for the few significant relationships between *sex-typing measures* and causal attributions.

1 Although we have conceptualized our experimental situation as a 'typical masculine achievement situation', it may well be that subjects have not perceived it as such. The anagrams task does not favour one sex or another. In future, the parameters of the task should be taken into consideration, as Deaux and Farris (1977) have demonstrated.

2 Masculinity and femininity are essential self-defining attributes for some people but not for others (Bem and Allen 1974). Perhaps if we had included in our study only those girls who consider it important to be feminine and those boys for whom masculinity is central to their self-concept, the hypothesized relationships between sex-typing and causal attributions would have been obtained.

A variable that was included in the context of the measure of sex-typing has demonstrated its utility in predicting the degree of ability attributions after failure: negative self-presentation was positively associated with lack of ability, in each of the eight subgroups (males and females), reaching significance in six of the eight groups. This result seems to suggest that lack of ability attributions are an indication of a more general tendency to present oneself in negative terms, irrespective of the particular content.

This brings us to another point: in our research, just as in

134

numerous other investigations, people are asked to make judgements that are the result of complex cognitive processes. In fact, they are asked to tell more than they know (Nisbett and Wilson 1977).

Nevertheless, people do make causal attributions, and in a sense it is surprising that they do so. How can you know why you succeeded or failed, if you performed the task only once, unless you can rely on certain general rules?

Kahneman and Tversky (1973) have demonstrated that people frequently make estimates of probability on the basis of judgements of similarity. For example, when attempting to assess the probability that a given individual is a librarian, people do not seek information about the proportion of librarians in the population (the statistical principle). Instead, they try to find out if the information they posses about the individual is representative (similar) to the stereotype they have about librarians. Nisbett and Wilson (1977) argue that such a 'representativeness heuristic' may also be employed by people when they seek to explain the causes of their own evaluations and behaviour. Thus, when people make causal attributions for failure and success, they should not primarily rely on the amount of correct solutions, but on the representativeness of the cause. Nisbett and Wilson (1977) state that a stimulus may be deemed a representative cause of a particular response for several reasons. For example the culture or subculture may supply explicit or implicit theories of causal relationships.

Thus, boys and girls may have different rules according to which they evaluate their successes and failures. Indeed, there exist some clear-cut sex stereotypes concerning causal attributions for a typical male and female (Deaux and Emswiller 1974; Etaugh and Hadley 1976; Feldman-Summers and Kiesler 1974) from an early age on.

If the causal attributions of our subjects are mainly the result of some general rule that is used among most subjects, we should not be surprised to find so few correlations between individual sex-typing and causal attribution, since there is evidence of only small correlations between sex-typing and perception of sex-role stereotypes (Spence *et al.* 1975). Also, we should be able to explain why there is no correlation between the number of correct solutions and ability attributions. This reasoning can contribute to an explanation of the findings of the present study, if one is willing to assume different subcultures in the four schools. In fact, different relationships between social desirability scores and certain achievement-related cognitions as a function of school and sex (see *Table 7(2)*) suggest a different perceived cultural demand.

Finally, more research is needed to investigate the effect of females' attributional patterns on various kinds of achievement behaviours, for instance females' career development. Certain effects can be predicted from Weiner's attributional model (1974). For instance, following Weiner, explanation of success by luck leads to less choice of achievement-related activities. If it can be shown that females' avoidance of achievement behaviour is mediated by their causal attributional patterns, it will be very important to change these causal attributions. Therefore, a greater understanding of the antecedents of causal attributions will also be necessary.

Summary

It was the purpose of the present research, first, to provide descriptive data on sex differences in causal attributions, and, second, to assess the relation between sex-typing, expectancy of success, and locus of control on the one hand and causal attributions on the other hand, for both males and females. The potential value of these variables in explaining sex differences in causal attributions was evaluated.

The subjects were 359 students (194 male, 165 female) from the last three years of four mixed-sex schools (fifteen to eighteen years). The Bem Sex Role Inventory (BSRI) was introduced as a measure of individual sex-typing and an adaptation of Rotter's locus of control scale was administered. After stating expectancies of success, subjects worked at ten six-letter anagrams for five minutes. Success and failure were manipulated through the use of easy and difficult anagrams. Then, subjects rated the degree to which they felt performance was due to ability, luck, effort, and task attributes. Results indicated that girls attributed their success more to luck and less to ability than boys; they also tended to show more luck attributions for failure.

There were large sex differences in attributions of lack of ability : in two schools, girls attributed their failure less to lack of ability than boys, while in the other two schools the reverse was true.

Although we are not able fully to explain this reversed sex difference across schools, we have gained some important information about the value of our hypothetic variables. Most notably sex differences in causal attributions – especially those of the failure condition – could not be explained by sex differences in initial expectations of success, in strong contradiction with the general expectancy interpretation. The lack of substantial relationships between individual sex-typing measures and causal attributions is discussed.

Another interpretation in terms of sex-role stereotypes is presented in this paper.

Acknowledgements

The author would like to thank Professor W. Claeys and Dr P. Deboeck for their helpful comments throughout the research. The author is also indebted to Dr B. Hopkins for his thoughtful suggestions and his assistance in correcting the English. Thanks are also extended to the school principals for their co-operation and to M. Van Dijck for her help in collecting the data.

References

ANDRIESSEN, J.H. (1972) Interne versus externe beheersing. *Nederlands Tijdschrift voor de psychologie en haar grensgebieden* 27:173-98.

BAR-TAL, D. and FRIEZE, I. (1977) Achievement motivation and gender as a determinant of attributions for success and failure. *Sex Roles* 3: 301-13.

BEM, S.L. (1974) The measurement of psychological androgyny. *Journal of Consulting and Clinical Psychology* 42:165-73

——(1975) Sex Role adaptability : one consequence of Psychological Androgyny. *Journal of Personality and Social Psychology* 31: 634-43.

BEM, D.J. and ALLEN, A. (1974) On predicting some of the people some of the time : the search for cross-situational consistencies in behaviour. *Psychological Review* 81:506-20

BEM, S.L. and LENNEY, E. (1976) Sextyping and the avoidance of cross-sex behaviour. *Journal of Personality and Social Psychology* 33:48-54.

BEM, S.L., MARTYNA, W., and WATSON, C. (1976) Sextyping and Androgyny : Further Explorations of the Expressive Domain. *Journal of Personality and Social Psychology* 34:1016-23.

DEAUX, K. and EMSWILLER, T. (1974) Explanations of successful performance on sex-linked tasks : what is skill for the male is luck for the female. *Journal of Personality and Social Psychology* 29:80-5.

137

DEAUX, K. and FARRIS, E. (1977) Attributing causes for one's own performance : the effects of sex, norms and task outcome. *Journal of Research in Personality* 11:59-72.

ETAUGH, C. and HADLEY, T. (1976) Causal Attributions of Male and Female Performance by Young Children. Paper presented at the XXIst International Congress of Psychology, Paris, July.

FEATHER, N.T. (1969) Attribution of responsibility and valence of success and failure in relation to initial confidence and task performance. *Journal of Personality and Social Psychology* 13:129-44.

FEATHER, N.T. and SIMON, J.G. (1971a) Causal attributions for success and failure in relation to expectations of success based upon selective and manipulative control. *Journal of Personality* 39:527-41.

——(1971b) Attributions of responsibility and valence of outcome in relation to initial confidence and success and failure of self and other. *Journal of Personality and Social Psychology* 18:173-88.

FELDMAN-SUMMERS, S. and KIESLER, S.B. (1974) Those who are number two try harder : the effect of sex on attributions of causality. *Journal of Personality and Social Psychology* 30:846-55.

FRIEZE, I. (1975) Women's expectations for and causal attributions of success and failure. In, M. Mednick, S. Tangri, and L. Hoffman (eds), *Women and Achievement : Social and Motivational Analyses.* Washington D.C.: Hemisphere Publishing Corporation.

FRIEZE, I., FISHER, J., HANUSA, B., McHUGHE, M.C., and VALLE, V.A. (in press). Attributions of the causes of success and failure as internal and external barriers to achievement in women. In, J. Sherman and F. Denmark (eds), *Psychology of Women : Future Directions of Research.* New York : Psychological Dimensions.

FRIEZE, I. and WEINER, B. (1971) Cue utilization and attributional judgements for success and failure. *Journal of Personality* 39:591-605.

KAHNEMAN, D. and TVERSKY, A. (1973) On the psychology of prediction. *Psychological Review* 80:237-51.

KERLINGER, F.N. and PEDHAZUR, E.J. (1973) *Multiple Regression in Behavioral Research.* New York: Holt, Rinehart and Winston.

LENNEY, E. (1977) Women's Self-Confidence in Achievement Settings. *Psychological Bulletin* 84:1-13.

MACCOBY, E.E. and JACKLIN, C.N. (1975) *The Psychology of Sex Differences.* Stanford, Calif.: Stanford University Press.

NISBETT, R.E. and WILSON, T.D. (1977) Telling more than we know : Selfperception and the representativeness heuristic. *Psychological Review* 84: 231-59.

ROSENFIELD, D. and STEPHAN, W.G. (1978) Sex differences in attributions for sex-typed tasks. *Journal of Personality* 46: 244-59.

ROTTER, J.B. (1966) Generalized expectancies for internal vs external control of reinforcement. *Psychological Monographs* 80:1-28.

SIMON, J.G. and FEATHER, N.T. (1973) Causal attribution for success and failure at university examinations. *Journal of Educational Psychology* 64:46-56.

SPENCE, J.T., HELMREICH, E., and STAFF, J. (1975) Ratings of self and peers on sex-role attributes and their relation to self-esteem and conceptions of masculinity and femininity. *Journal of Personality and Social Psychology* 32:29-39.

STEIN, A.H. and BAILEY, M.H. (1973) The socialization of achievement orientation in females. *Psychological Bulletin* 80:345-66.

VALLE, V.A. and FRIEZE, I.H. (1976) The stability of causal attributions as a mediator in changing expectations for success. *Journal of Personality and Social Psychology* 33:579-87.

VIAENE, N. (1977) Measuring psychological androgyny with the BSRI, some findings and critical comments. University of Leuven (unpublished manuscript).

WEINER, B. (1974) *Achievement Motivation and Attribution Theory.* Morristown, N.J.: General Learning Press.

WEINER, B., HECHAUSEN, H., MEYER, W.V., and COOK, E.E. (1972) Causal ascriptions and achievement motivation : a conceptual analysis of effort and reanalysis of locus of control. *Journal of Personality and Social Psychology* 21:239-48.

tive situations with men. Horner actually tested women on maths and verbal skills, alone and in mixed sex competition, and found that subjects low in fear of success (FOS) performed significantly better under competitive circumstances than when alone, while the reverse was true for high FOS women. The conceptualization of this motive, formulated within the context of the Expectancy-Value theory (Atkinson and Feather 1966), as an additional factor in the overall assessment of achievement motivation was an important step towards explaining the previous inconsistent results in the investigation of achievement motivation in women.

Since then, Horner's research has attracted the attention of researchers in various areas of social science, and a formidable number of investigations attempting replication and expansion of experimental design, redefinition of theoretical constructs, and novel perspectives on the M–s have resulted in confusion, misconceptions, and the accumulation of disjointed, if not contradictory, empirical evidence. This paper aims to lend structure to the burgeoning collection of literature concerning fear of success and to place the research within its original context of motivational theory. To explain M–s in these terms, the assessment and measurement of fear of success is presented in conjunction with earlier research on achievement motivation. The paper concentrates on three areas:

1 Methodological and theoretical criticisms of M–s research (validity and reliability of measurement, fear of success as a situational variable, M–s as a reflection of sex-role stereotypes),
2 Explanation of M–s within the Expectancy-Value theory of motivation and supporting research, and
3 Suggestions for further research.

Criticisms of M–s

Horner's postulations concerning the motive to avoid success in women have induced a mass of empirical data, as yet unsynthesized, and several major criticisms of its motivational conceptualization, assessment, and application. The most frequent criticisms centre on the unconventional development of the projective assessment and the potentially unreliable nature of the measurement technique. The establishment of fear of success as an independent motivational component has also been questioned, with opponents maintaining that it should be viewed as a situational variable or as merely reflective of contemporary sex-role stereotypes.

Tresemer (1974;1976) and Shaver (1976) note that Horner did not adopt the conventional method of establishing and isolating a motive. Typically, projective stories from an aroused group form the basis of a scoring system that is applied to themes from a neutral group. In the traditional sense Horner did not compare themes of aroused and neutral groups but, rather, established her own criteria. Stories were scored motive present if they exhibited negative affect toward success, instrumental activity away from success, anticipation of negative consequences because of success, denial of effort or situation, or bizarre, non-adaptive responses (Horner 1972). However, Horner's criteria appeared valid as fear of success imagery emerged as a consistent predictor of behavioural responses in achievement oriented situations. In particular, women displaying FOS imagery in projective responses performed significantly worse on maths and verbal skills in competitive circumstances than alone.

Projective assessment of the motive to avoid success is also criticized for its potential unreliability. With no extensive scoring manual available and a simple present/absent procedure, a substantial subjective element necessarily comes into play. Although the test-retest reliability of 0.73 reported by Moore (1974) appears substantial, as does the intertester reliability estimated at 0.80 to 0.90 by Zuckerman and Wheeler (1975), there is a wide variation in FOS imagery over studies. This may be partially accounted for by the fact that females have a tendency to score stories 'motive-present' more often than males (Robbins and Robbins 1973). However, with homogeneity of scorers reliability for fantasy-based measures of achievement motivation calculated at only 0.30 to 0.40 (Entwisle 1972), it is difficult to attribute reported discrepancies to treatment effects or method variance. The fact that most researchers have found a low or non-existent correspondence over cues suggests that method variance may be a confounding factor (Weston and Mednick 1970; Morgan and Mausner 1973; Alper 1974; Karabenick and Marshall 1974; Tresemer 1974).

But given the potential unreliability of the measurement, how does the motive to avoid success stand up under test conditions? One of Horner's basic tenets is that women exhibiting M–s feel unsexed by success, and experience the most anxiety in competition with men. Murphy-Berman (1975; 1976) attempted to test this underlying assumption by questioning women after they had been engaged in competitive tasks. FOS subjects did not estimate that their partners wanted to be with them less after success than failure, nor that these males viewed them as less feminine after success. Nevertheless, Makosky (1972), Parker (1972), and Sorrentino and Short (1974) discovered that FOS women perform optimally on a task labelled feminine.

Horner asserts that women who manifest M–s perform worse in competition with men than with other women or working alone. This has been empirically demonstrated by Hyatt, Cooper, and Allen (1970), Groszko and Morganstern (cited in Makosky 1972), Makosky (1972), Parker (1972), Allen and Boivan (1976), and Romer (1977). Further support is offered by Karabenick and Marshall (1974) and Karabenick, Marshall, and Karabenick (1976) who found that women who are high in both fear of success and fear of failure depress performances in competitive situations. Similarly, Patty (1976) found that high FOS women performed better than low FOS women on digit-span tasks when the instructional set described the task as easy whereas low FOS women rendered superior performances when the task was described as moderately difficult. Zaro (1972) reported that women who are high in FOS react more co-operatively in competitive circumstances than low FOS women; likewise, Bongort (1974) found high FOS women more co-operative in the Prisoner's Dilemma, a forced choice decision-making task that allows exploitative and co-operative responses with the reward outcomes dependent upon the opponent's simultaneous manoeuvre. However, results from Karabenick (1972), Althof (1973), Feather and Simon (1973), Morgan and Mausner (1973), and Zanna (1973) do not reflect these trends.

A further criticism of FOS investigation comes from those researchers who have expanded the original Horner design to allow both sexes to respond to male and female stimulus persons (SPs). Results have been inconclusive although the majority of studies report FOS imagery most prevalent in response to a female SP (Prescott 1971; Feather and Simon 1973; Wellens 1973; Alper 1974; Brown, Jennings, and Vanik 1974; Feather and Raphelson

143

1974; Monahan, Kuhn, and Shaver 1974; Winchel, Fenner, and Shaver 1974; Solomon 1975; Jackaway and Teevan 1976). However Katz (1973), Kimball (1973), Krusell (1973), Robbins and Robbins (1973), Hoffman (1974), Jackaway (1974), Tresemer (1974), Levine and Crumrine (1975), and Wood and Greenfeld (1976), found no significant difference in the proportion of FOS imagery in response to male and female stimulus persons. The former group of investigators, supported by Zuckerman and Wheeler (1975), maintain that projective techniques for the assessment of M–s may be merely tapping sex-role stereotypes rather than providing a valid motivational measurement. This is because men tend to respond with very high proportions of negative imagery to female cues, while females produce predominantly positive stories for male cues.

Although these studies yield interesting results, in terms of assessment of motivation sex appropriateness of stimulus person is a crucial factor. A consistent body of research on measurement and development of achievement motivation has been derived from male subjects in response to male Thematic Apperception Test (TAT) figures (Atkinson 1958). But responses of female subjects to male TAT figures do not conform to the same patterns. French and Lesser (1964), Veroff, Wilcox, and Atkinson (1953), and Wilcox (1951) found that although achievement imagery in women was greater in response to male pictures, it did not increase in achievement-oriented situations. Nor do female cues accurately measure achievement motivation in males. Veroff (1950) found that achievement imagery is low for high school males in response to female pictures, and that there is little change from neutral to aroused conditions. In this instance, McClelland, Atkinson, Clark, and Lowell (1953) concluded that 'male pictures provide a measurement of achievement motivation, female pictures do not' (p. 168). They do not conclude that the measurement of achievement motivation is merely reflective of sex-role stereotypes *because* males respond with less achievement imagery to female cues.

Indeed, if motivational assessment is based on identification and projection as suggested by Atkinson (1958), presentation of a same sex SP is most appropriate in facilitating this process. By contrast, being able to rely on extrinsic factors, e.g. stereotypes, is more probable when responding, to a cross-sexed SP. This does not mean that measurement of achievement motivation by projective techniques solely delineates the pervading sex-role stereotypes, but rather that an appropriate stimulus is required to obtain a valid response.

The importance of a sex-appropriate SP is further corroborated by Murray (1943) in the development of the TAT technique: 'Experience has shown that in the long run the stories obtained are more revealing and the validity of the interpretations increased if most of the pictures include a person who is of the same sex as the subject' (p. 2). The importance of this factor has been demonstrated empirically by Wayner and Lindskold (1976) : subjects project more of their own characteristics on SPs they believe to be similar to themselves.

Finally, there is the argument proposed by Condry and Dyer (1976) that fear of success should be considered as a situational rather than a motivational variable. This rests on the assumption that social norms imply the existence of an extrinsic social-reward structure, positively rewarding acceptance of norms and actively punishing deviation. In these terms, fear of success is seen as a set of realistic expectancies concerning the negative consequences of deviancy from a set of cultural norms of sex-appropriate behaviour. This is corroborated by Argote, Fisher, McDonald, and O'Neil (1976), who found that females who were rejected after success or accepted after failure in competition with men performed significantly worse on subsequent tasks than those who were accepted after success or rejected after failure. While this argument is plausible, it is not antithetical with Horner's notion of M–s. The discrepancy lies in the tendency for Condry and Dyer to dismiss FOS as merely a reflection of realistic expectations while Horner maintains that these expectancies are incorporated into personality dispositions and directly affect motivation.

The latter two criticisms reflect a naïve and simplistic approach to achievement motivation and a misunderstanding of the Expectancy-Value theory from which M–s is derived. Atkinson and Feather's (1966) theory of achievement motivation states that the strength of one's motivation to achieve success (T s) is a product of the multiplication of the strength of the motive to succeed (M s), the expectancy of success (P s), and the incentive value of success (I s) : $T s = M s \times P s \times I s$. The motive refers to a latent disposition to strive for a particular goal, state, or aim. Expectancies concerning success reflect the *probability* that the performance will induce a specific consequence and the *incentive* or value, the type and magnitude of reward. While the motive *per se* may be relatively stable, expectancies are situational; therefore, total motivation and, consequently, achievement performance will vary as the motivational components alter. Atkinson refers to motivation as the aroused state that exists when a motive has been engaged by the appropriate expectancy – i.e. that performance of an act is instrumental to attainment of the goal of the motive.

The relationship, then, between motive and performance is not simple or direct. Atkinson and Reitman (1956) have demonstrated that a correspondence between M s and performance is only consistent when the former is accompanied by positive expectancies. If other motives such as affiliation or power are aroused in conjunction with the achievement motive, the positive correlation further deteriorates.

According to Atkinson (1958), total motivation for performance of an act will be the sum of the contributions made by particular motives engaged. In the case of achievement motivation (T a) both the motivation towards success (T s) and the motivation to avoid failure (T–f) are considered important contributors to the overall manifestation. Within this framework, a consistent body of data has been established on the sources, measurement, and development of achievement motivation in men. But the framework is incomplete in that it neither explains sex differences nor distinguishes between competitive and non-competitive situations. To alleviate this deficiency, Horner postulates that the measurement of achievement motivation should incorporate the motive to avoid success. This can be expressed mathematically as: $T a = (Ts - T–f) - T–s$.

Explanation of the theory of achievement motivation in a broader context unveils inherent misconceptions in the 'stereotype' and 'situational' criticisms of the motive to avoid success. Horner conceptualizes the motive as a stable personality disposition acquired early in life in conjunction with sex-role standards. It is precisely the stereotypic notions of masculinity/femininity and success-related ideology that influence *expectancies* about achievement behaviour. In particular, women learn to fear success in anticipation of negative consequences: loss of femininity and social desirability. These expectancies, a prime motivational component, decrease the value of success. Condry and Dyer (1976) refer to fear of success as 'realistic expectancies about the negative consequences of deviancy from a set of cultural norms of sex appropriate behaviour' (p. 71), and advocate its consideration as a situational variable without the apparent realization that the situational nature of these expectancies is already accounted for in comprehensive motivational terms and that their proposition is not antithetical with Horner's conceptualization.

Support for M–s

VARIATION IN CUES AND SUBJECTS

Horner's original cue contained three main components: *female success* in a *competitive, male-dominated* field. Several studies have examined responses to variation in the cue and there is a tendency for FOS to alter in stereotypic fashion. Breedlove and Cicirelli (1974) assessed the M–s in response to female achievement in medicine and education and found the proportion of FOS significantly higher in the first instance. Lockheed (1975) found that the proportion of FOS diminished in response to a female cue when the medical school class was described as 50 per cent female. It appears that when an occupation is defined as deviant for women, a higher percentage of FOS imagery is elicited. However, Hoffman (1974) presented students with three variations of Horner's cue: a less masculine field (child psychology), achievement communicated privately, and competition minimized. None of these variables diminished FOS. Variations in extraneous factors in cue have also been investigated and apparently affect the proportion of FOS imagery. For example, Spence's (1974) research indicates that marital status of a female SP may affect the quality and quantity of FOS imagery.

For the most part women are found to evince more FOS than men (Horner 1968; 1972; Feather and Simon 1973; Monahan *et al.* 1974; Prescott 1971), although Levine and Crumrine (1973) and Morgan and Mausner (1973) reported a higher proportion of FOS in the latter. Likewise, white women appear more prone to FOS than blacks. Horner (1972) and Weston and Mednick (1970) reported less FOS imagery in black than white women. Puryear and Mednick (1974) also found FOS less prevalent in blacks. These results appear to be consistent with the view of the black

147

matriarchal society in which women are thought to be more autonomous. Black men, on the other hand, display greater proportions of FOS than either white men or black women (Horner 1972). Interestingly, Puryear and Mednick also found that M–s was associated with militant black attitudes, particularly in those women who had no attachment to a man. This has been interpreted as dependent upon the acceptance, by militant blacks, of white middle-class ideology, including the role and status of women.

Feather and Raphelson's (1974) cross-cultural study revealed a higher incidence of FOS in Australian university women (47 per cent) as compared with American women (27 per cent). It has been suggested that the more rigid stereotypes maintained in Australia may be conducive to greater FOS in these women. Weinreich-Haste (1978) reported 44.5 per cent FOS in a British sample. Although little research has appeared in the area, Ward's (1976; 1977) investigations suggest that FOS patterns in Britain generally reflect American trends. In a series of experiments with university women responding to a sex-appropriate cue FOS ranged from 40 per cent (nursing) to 57.7 per cent (botany) with intermediate samples of 52 per cent (engineering) and 54.8 per cent (medicine). Even greater proportions of negative imagery (up to 67.5 per cent) arose from male responses to female SPs. Fear of success was also prevalent in a sample of professional women (cue: acting head of medical school), but was not consistently related to self-concept (psychological androgyny), attitudes toward women, or personal history factors.

FOS does appear to be positively correlated with age, beginning in early adolescence and increasing with highlighted sexual awareness. Baruch (1975) established an increase in FOS imagery in students from fifth to tenth grade (ten to fifteen years old). This is corroborated by Lavach and Lanier (1975) with seventh- and tenth-grade samples, Horner and Rhoem (1968) with seventh- and eleventh-grade subjects, and Kimball and Leahy (1976) with fourth- to tenth-grade children.

But investigations of the relationship between academic concentration and the M–s have yielded contradictory results. Horner (1969) and Patty (1972) found a concentration of FOS females in traditional fields. Horner reported 89 per cent FOS stories from women in traditional areas as opposed to 43 per cent from those in non-traditional endeavours. However, Gearty and

148

Milner (1975) found no relation between M–s and academic concentration, nor did Moore (1972) who tested women in law, nursing, graduate arts, and sciences. The M–s has been reported to be more prevalent in honour students (Horner 1974), women of high academic ability (Hoffman 1974; Kresojevich 1972; Sorrentino and Short 1974), and females attending coeducational institutions (Winchel, Fenner, and Shaver 1974).

FOS AND PERSONALITY

Because Horner maintains that the M–s is a stable personality disposition, various attempts have been made to correlate FOS with specific personality traits and personal attitudes and ambitions. Patty (1972) found that although high FOS women are highly career oriented, they lack actual dedication. They are most frequently concentrated in traditional occupations and commonly display feelings of self-inadequacy and self-criticism. Parker (1972) discovered that high FOS women view home and family as most important while low FOS women place great emphasis on career orientation. Although this seems contradictory at first glance, these results neatly fit into Horner's con cepualization of FOS. High FOS women must view home and family as valuable in order to experience the role conflict that inhibits achievement motivation. In addition, high FOS women are also characterized by their academic competence and career orientation. It is the combination of the ability and the ideological acceptance of the traditional female role that produces the achievement-related anxiety. Along these lines, women who score low in FOS view themselves as more feminine (Makosky 1972; Parker 1972). Again, it seems that conflict appears in high FOS women because they perceive their own self-concepts as transgressing traditional sex-role norms. However, contrary to expectation, Baruch (1975) found that women who are low in FOS produce higher stereotype scores, while Alper (1974), Esposito (1977), and Tresemer and Pleck (1972) related high FOS to traditional stereotyping and attitudes.

In practical application to the academic setting, Curtis, Zanna, and Campbell (1975) reported that females displaying the M–s are less satisfied with law school and very reluctant to volunteer answers in class. Along these lines Horner (1972) found that girls evincing FOS experienced anxiety about success and

149

refused to divulge the fact that they were doing well academically. Sixty-seven per cent were more willing to tell their boyfriends that they had received an average than a superior mark, whereas 100 per cent of those low in FOS would more likely report the superior performance. Schwenn (1970) suggests that the major role in the arousal of FOS is played by girls' male peers, and this is supported by Peplau (1976) who found that a combination of FOS and traditional sex-role attitudes adversely affects competitive performances against boyfriends. Similarly, Depner and O'Leary (1976) reported that women who perceive the significant males in their lives as endorsing non-traditional gender role behaviour are more likely to respond negatively to vicarious success and Schnitzer (1977) found that subjects who composed FOS stories to achievement-oriented cues were more likely to produce negative responses to affiliative cues, fearing emotional pain.

On the whole, although results are not conclusive, empirical trends tend to support Horner's conceptualization of M–s as a debilitating anxiety in achievement-oriented situations. There is a tendency for FOS to be most frequently elicited by female success in male-dominated fields and to be more apparent in psychologically feminine women. The conflict between success and femininity and a decline in achievement-oriented behaviour is most apparent in competition with men in specifically masculine endeavours. There is also a tendency for M–s to emerge in puberty and increase with heightened sex-role awareness. In short, sex-role learning adversely affects achievement motivation in women.

Directions for further research

For the most part researchers have devoted much time to amassing empirical data and neglecting its critical synthesis into a comprehensive motivational theory. Despite ever-increasing masses of literature devoted to fear of success it is difficult to assess the current status of M–s. In this light, several criticisms and suggestions can be made.

1 Although the use of projective techniques is intrinsically subject to criticisms of validity and reliability, a more extensive scoring manual for M–s is required. Only then can large discrepancies in the proportion of FOS imagery among

studies be attributed to treatment effects rather than measuremental unreliability.

2 For a valid measurement of achievement motivation, sex-appropriate SPs are required. Responses to cross-sexed SPs may reflect 'attitudes' about success and failure but do not necessarily index motives.

3 The M–s should be considered within the context of the Expectancy-Value theory of motivation. Naïve and simplistic attempts to relate FOS imagery to personality, attitudes, and performance will be largely unsuccessful : emphasis should be switched from *imagery* to *motive*.

4 More research should be devoted to the relationship between M–s and performance. Results, to date, are not conclusive and the establishment of a reliable relationship would argue for the validation of M–s as an independent component of achievement motivation.

References

ALLEN, J.L. and BOIVAN, M. (1976) Women's will to fail in a disjunctive reaction time competitive task. *Bulletin of the Psychonomic Society* 8(15):4012.

ALPER, T. (1974) Achievement motivation in college women. *American Psychologist* 29:194-203.

ALTHOF, S.E. (1973) *The effects of competitive and noncompetitive conditions in high and low fear of success college women on verbal problem solving ability*. Oklahoma State University, Stillwater (unpublished master's thesis). Cited by J. Condry and S. Dyer (1976) Attribution of cause to the victim. *Journal of Social Issues* 32(3):63-83.

ARGOTE, L.M., FISHER, J.E., McDONALD, P.J., and O'NEIL, E.C. (1976) Competitiveness in males and females: Situational determinants of fear of success behaviour. *Sex Roles* 2(3):295-303.

ATKINSON, J.W. (ed.) (1958) *Motives in Fantasy, Action and Society*. New York: Van Nostrand.

ATKINSON, J.W. and FEATHER, N.T. (eds) (1966) *A Theory of Achievement Motivation*. New York: Wiley.

ATKINSON, J.W. and REITMAN, W. (1956) Performance as a function of motive strength and expectancy of goal attainment. *Journal of Abnormal and Social Psychology* 53:361-66.

BARUCH, G. (1975) Sex role stereotyping, the motive to avoid success and parental identification. *Sex Roles* 1(4):303-9.

BONGORT, K.J. (1974) Expressions of fear of success in the prisoner's dilemma games as played by male and female pairs. University of

Michigan (unpublished manuscript). Cited by J. Condry and S. Dyer (1976).

BREEDLOVE, C. and CICIRELLI, V. (1974) Women's fear of success in relation to personal characteristics and type of occupation. *Journal of Psychology* 86:181-90.

BROWN, M., JENNINGS, J., and VANIK, V. (1974) The motive to avoid success: A further examination. *Journal of Research in Personality* 8:172-76.

CONDRY, J. and DYER, S. (1976) Attribution of cause to the victim. *Journal of Social Issues* 32(3):63-83.

CURTIS, R., ZANNA, M., and CAMPBELL, W. (1975) Sex, fear of success and perceptions and performance of law school students. *American Educational Research Journal* 12(3):287-97.

DEPNER, C., and O'LEARY, V. (1976) Understanding female careerism: Fear of success and new directions. *Sex Roles* 2(3):259-68.

ENTWISLE, D.R. (1972) To dispel fantasies about fantasy based measures of achievement motivation. *Psychological Bulletin* 77:377-91.

ESPOSITO, R.P. (1977) The relationship between the motive to avoid success and vocational choice. *Journal of Vocational Behaviour* 10:347-57.

FEATHER, N.T. and RAPHELSON, A. (1974) Fear of success in Australian and American student groups: Motive or sex role stereotype? *Journal of Personality* 42:190-201.

FEATHER, N.T. and SIMON, J. (1973) Fear of success and causal attribution for outcome. *Journal of Personality* 41(4):525-41.

FRENCH, E. and LESSER, G.S. (1964) Some characteristics of the achievement motive in women. *Journal of Abnormal and Social Psychology* 68(2):119-28.

GEARTY, J. and MILNER, J. (1975) Academic major, gender of examiner and motive to avoid success in women. *Journal of Clinical Psychology* 31(1):13-14.

HOFFMAN, L. (1974) Fear of success imagery in males and females: 1965 and 1971. *Journal of Consulting and Clinical Psychology* 42(3):353-58.

HORNER, M.S. (1968) *Sex differences in achievement motivation and performance in competitive and noncompetitive situations* (Doctoral dissertation, University of Michigan). Ann Arbor, Michgan: University Microfilms.

——(1969) Fail: Bright women. *Psychology Today* 3:36-8.

——(1972) Motive to avoid success and changing aspirations of women. In, J. Bardwick (ed.), *Readings on the Psychology of Women*. New York: Harper and Row.

——(1974) The measurement and behavioral implications of fear of success in women. In, J. Atkinson and J. Raynor (eds) *Motivation and Achievement*. New York: Wiley.

HORNER, M.S. and RHOEM, W. (1968) The motive to avoid success as a function of age, occupation and progress at school. University of Michigan (unpublished manuscript).

HYATT, F.A., COOPER, G.G., and ALLEN, J.L. (1970) The motive to avoid success in a disjunctive reaction time competitive task. Spring Arbor College (unpublished manuscript). Cited by J. Condry and S. Dyer (1976).

JACKAWAY, R. (1974) Sex differences in the development of fear of success. *Child Study Journal* 4(2):71-9.

JACKAWAY, R. and TEEVAN, R. (1976) Fear of failure and fear of success: Two dimensions of the same motive. *Sex Roles* 2(3):283-93.

KARABENICK, S.A. (1972) The effect of sex of competition on the performance of females following success. Paper presented at the Annual Meeting of the American Psychological Association.

KARABENICK, S.A. and MARSHALL, J.M. (1974) Performance of females as a function of fear of success, fear of failure, type of opponent and performance contingent feedback. *Journal of Personality* 42:220-37.

KARABENICK, S.A., MARSHALL, J.M., and KARABENICK, J.D. (1976) Effects of fear of success, fear of failure, type of opponent and feedback on female achievement performance. *Journal of Research in Personality* 10:369-85.

KATZ, M.L. (1973) Female motive to avoid success: A psychological barrier or a response to deviancy? ETS, Princeton (unpublished manuscript). Cited by J. Condry and S. Dyer (1976).

KIMBALL, B. and LEAHY, R.L. (1976) Fear of success in males and females: Effects of developmental level and sex linked course of study. *Sex Roles* 2(3):273-81.

KIMBALL, M. (1973) Women and success: A basic conflict? Paper presented at the Society for Research in Child Development Convention, Philadelphia.

KRESOJEVICH, I.Z. (1972) Motivation to avoid success in women as related to year in school, academic achievement and success content. *Dissertation Abstracts International* 33:2348-349.

KRUSELL, J.L. (1973) Attribution of responsibility for performance attempts of males and females. University of Rochester (unpublished doctoral dissertation). Cited by J. Condry and S. Dyer (1976) Attribution of cause to the victim. *Journal of Social Issues* 32(3):63-83.

LAVACH, J. and LANIER, H. (1975) The motive to avoid success in 7th, 8th, 9th, and 10th grade high achieving girls. *Journal of Educational Research* 68(6):216-18

LEVINE, A. and CRUMRINE, J. (1975) Women and the fear of success. *American Journal of Sociology* 80(4):964-74.

LOCKHEED, M. (1975) Female motive to avoid success: A psychological barrier or a response to deviancy? *Sex Roles* 1(1):41-50.

MAKOSKY, V. (1972) Fear of success, sex role orientation of task and competitive conditions as variables affecting performance in achievement oriented situations. St Lawrence University (unpublished manuscript).

153

McCLELLAND, D., ATKINSON, J.W., CLARK, R., and LOWELL, E. (1953) *The Achievement Motive*. New York: Appleton-Century-Crofts.

MONAHAN, L., KUHN, D., and SHAVER, P. (1974) Intra-psychic vs. cultural explanations of the 'fear of success' motive. *Journal of Personality and Social Psychology* **29**(1):60-4.

MOORE, K. (1974) Fear of success: The distribution, correlates, reliability and consequences for fertility of fear of success among respondents in a metropolitan survey population. Paper presented at the Annual Meeting of the American Psychological Association, New Orleans.

MOORE, L. (1972) The relationship of academic group membership to motive to avoid success in women. *Dissertation Abstracts International* **32**(8):4355.

MORGAN, S.W. and MAUSNER, B. (1973) Behavioural and fantasized indicators of avoidance of success in men and women. *Journal of Personality* **41**:457-70.

MURPHY-BERMAN, V. (1975) Motive to avoid success: A test of basic assumptions. *Representative Research in Social Psychology* **6**:37-44.

—— (1976) Effects of success and failure on perception of gender identity. *Sex Roles* **2**(4):367-74.

MURRAY, H.A. (1943) *Thematic Apperception Test Manual*. Cambridge, Mass.: Harvard University Press.

PARKER, V. (1972) Fear of success, sex role orientation of task and competition as variables affecting women's performance in achievement oriented situations. *Dissertation Abstracts International* **32**(9b):5495.

PATTY, R.A. (1972) Female motive to avoid success: Delimiting the population. University of Nebraska, Lincoln (unpublished research report).

PATTY, R.A. (1976) The motive to avoid success and instructional set. *Sex Roles* **2**(1):81-3.

PEPLAU, L.A. (1976) Impact of fear of success and sex role attitudes on women's competitive performance. *Journal of Personality and Social Psychology* **34**(4):561-64.

PRESCOTT, D. (1971) Efficacy-related imagery, education and politics. Harvard University (unpublished honours thesis). Cited by J. Condry and S. Dyer (1976).

PURYEAR, G. and MEDNICK, M. (1974) Black militancy, affective attachment and fear of success in black college women. *Journal of Consulting and Clinical Psychology* **42**(2):263-66.

ROBBINS, L. and ROBBINS, E. (1973) Comment on 'Toward an understanding of achievement related conflicts.' *Journal Social Issues* **29**: 133-37.

ROMER, N. (1977) Sex related differences in the motive to avoid success, sex role identity and performance in competitive and noncompetitive conditions. *Psychology of Women Quarterly* **1**(3):260-72.

SCHNITZER, P.K. (1977) The motive to avoid success; Exploring the nature of the fear. *Psychology of Women Quarterly* **1**(3):273-82.

SCHWENN, M. (1970) Arousal of the motive to avoid success. Harvard

University (unpublished honours thesis).

SHAVER, P. (1976) Questions concerning fear of success and its conceptual relatives. *Ses Roles* 2(3):305-20.

SOLOMON, L. (1975) The perception of a successful person of the same or the opposite sex. *Journal of Social Psychology* 95:133-34.

SORRENTINO, R. and SHORT, J. (1974) Effects of fear of success on women's performance at masculine vs. feminine tasks. *Journal of Research in Personality* 8:277-90.

SPENCE, J.T. (1974) The TAT and attitudes toward achievement in women. *Journal of Consulting and Clinical Psychology* 42(3):427-37.

TRESEMER, D. (1974) Fear of success: Popular but unproven. *Psychology Today* (7): 82-5.

——(1976) Do women fear success? *Signs* 1(4): 863-75.

TRESEMER, D. and PLECK, J. (1972) Maintaining and changing sex role boundaries in men and women. Paper presented at Women: Resource for a Changing World Conference, Radcliffe.

VEROFF, J. (1950) A projective measure of achievement motivation in adolescent males and females. Wesleyan University (unpublished honours thesis). Cited by D. McClelland, J.W. Atkinson, R. Clark, and E. Lowell (eds) (1953).

VEROFF, J., WILCOX, S., and ATKINSON, J.W. (1953) The achievement motive in high school and college age women. *Journal of Abnormal and Social Psychology* 48:108-19.

WARD, C. (1976) Fear of success and antifeminism in university women. Paper presented at Durham Post-Graduate Conference in Psychology, Durham.

——(1977) *Explorations in sex role stereotypes* University of Durham (unpublished doctoral thesis).

WAYNER, M. and LINDSKOLD, S. (1976) Stereotypes, projection and attraction. *Journal of Social Psychology* 99:301-2.

WEINREICH-HASTE, H. (1978) Sex differences in 'fear of success' among British students. *British Journal of Social and Clinical Psychology* 17:37-42.

WELLENS, G. (1973) The motive to avoid success in high school seniors – need for achievement and psychosocial correlates. *Dissertation Abstracts International* 33(2b):5529.

WESTON, P. and MEDNICK, M. (1970) Race, social class and the motive to avoid success in women. *Journal of Cross-cultural Psychology*. 1(3):284-91.

WILCOX, S. (1951) A projective measure of achievement motivation of college women. University of Michigan (unpublished honours thesis).

WINCHEL, R., FENNER, D., and SHAVER, P. (1974) Impact of coeducation on 'fear of success' imagery expressed by male and female high school students. *Journal of Educational Psychology* 66(5):726-30.

WOOD, M.M. and GREENFELD, S.T. (1976) Women managers and fear of success: A study in the field. *Sex Roles* 2(4):375-87.

ZANNA, M.P. (1973) Intellectual competition and the female student. Report to the US Department of Health, Education and Welfare. Cited by M. Zuckerman and L. Wheeler (1975).

ZARO, J. (1972) An experimental study of role conflict in women. *Dissertation Abstracts International* 33(6b):2828.

ZUCKERMAN, M. and WHEELER, L. (1975) To dispel fantasies about fantasy based measures of fear of success. *Psychological Bulletin* 82(6):932-46.

PART FOUR

Education

NINE

Sex differences in examination performance: do these reflect differences in ability or sex-role stereotypes?

ROGER J.L. MURPHY

Introduction

The well-known phenomenon that, within the years of secondary education, girls tend to prefer arts subjects and boys tend to prefer science subjects is reflected in the General Certificate of Education (GCE) examination statistics. *Table 9(1)* gives a breakdown of the cumulative figures for all the GCE Boards, comparing the number of entries from and performance of male and female candidates in a selection of eight major 'O' level subjects in the June 1976 examinations. Greater differences can be found in other subjects such as Cookery and Metalwork, but they have a lower entry than the subjects shown.

These eight 'O' level subjects show the conventional sex differentiated trends in terms of the relative number of males and females entering each subject. However, apart from Biology, which, as far as sex differences are concerned, always appears to be the odd one out of the sciences (Ormerod 1975), it is noticeable that the pass rates for males and females in the male-dominated science subjects are very similar, while in the female-dominated (Arts) subjects the female pass rate is higher than the male. This may, to some extent, reflect the general tendency for better all-round female attainment at this level of education (Monday et al. 1967).

In this paper we propose to investigate further these sex differences in both subject choice and performance on examinations in different subjects. We shall investigate these differences from a number of different angles, and in particular we shall discuss whether they can be considered to be the result of differences in ability between the sexes or whether they are more a function of sex-role stereotyping.

Sex differences in intellectual functioning

There are areas of intellectual functioning that have traditionally been thought of as displaying consistent differences between the sexes, and there is a possible link-up between these and the differences in examination performance. There is, however, considerable controversy over the interpretation of the great mass of research studies that have attempted to investigate these possible differences. Maccoby and Jacklin (1975) provided an extensive analysis of over 1,400 such studies published since 1965, and on this basis rejected a number of commonly held beliefs about sex differences. They did, however, conclude that sex differences in verbal ability, visual-spatial ability, and quantitative ability are fairly well established (girls, they claim, excel in verbal ability, whereas boys excel in visual-spatial and quantitative ability). However, Maccoby and Jacklin's book has been strongly criticized (e.g. by Block 1976 and Fairweather 1976) both for the conclusions drawn from the studies that it does report, and for the fact that it missed out so much important work. Block rounded off her criticisms by saying that, 'The long, arduous, complicated evaluation process undertaken by the authors in their effort to impose organization upon a sprawling, unruly body of data is vulnerable to error and reasonable argument at every step along the way' (Block 1976:522). Fairweather was more

160

Table 9(1) *Comparison of male and female entries and pass rates in various GCE 'O' level examinations in* June 1976 *(all boards)*

Subject	Sex	Entry	% obtaining ABC grades
English Literature*	Females	141,000	64
	Males	106,000	54
English Language*	Females	203,000	65
	Males	183,000	56
French*	Females	84,000	64
	Males	66.000	58
Religious Studies*	Females	40,000	63
	Males	25,000	51
Chemistry**	Females	30,000	60
	Males	60,000	61
Physics**	Females	25,000	58
	Males	86,000	59
Mathematics**	Females	87,000	56
	Males	116,000	60
Biology†	Females	86,000	56
	Males	61,000	61

*   Higher female entry and pass rate.
**   Higher male entry and pass rate.
†   Higher female entry. Higher male pass rate.

concerned that, 'Much of the European and notably British literature is missing; regrettably so, since studies here seem much less prone to spectacular findings, especially in childhood' (Fairweather 1976:234).

All of this goes to demonstrate the point that great uncertainty exists in this area, and it is dangerous to assume at the present time that there are such things as clearly established sex differences in intellectual functioning. Certainly differences have been reported, and some differences have occurred in a variety of studies, but the consistency of these occurrences is not great enough to allow sweeping conclusions to be drawn. Sex differences in the results of experimental studies may easily occur as

161

artifacts of individual experiments, either because of the particular methods used or because of the way that subjects have been selected. Thus, only where consistent differences can be found across experimental situations is it possible to draw general conclusions about their existence amongst the members of the two sexes. A related point to this is one made by Saraga (1975) and Dwyer (1976), who go to great lengths to emphasize the need to realize the amount of overlap that exists when studies of intellectual functioning do show significant differences between the average scores of males and females. These authors also point out that there is normally more variation in these skills within groups of males or females than there ever is between them.

If one does consider the possibility of the existence of sex differences in intellectual functioning, there is still the question to be asked as to whether they are the result of some innate biologically determined sex differences or whether they are the result of the influence of culturally defined sex-role stereotypes. Hutt (1974) argues that socio-cultural expectations are certainly important, but she has it that these must have come from somewhere, and she argues that they must at least be based on some basic inherent differences between the sexes. On the other hand, Glickman (1976) after considering several possible physiological theories, such as different rates of development of males and females, brain lateralization, and the influence of sex hormones, concludes that cultural reinforcement on its own is the most realistic reason for these sex differences in intellectual functioning.

The question as to how stereotypes of sex differences in intellectual functioning arise is also raised by Bee (1974) and is clearly a central issue in this debate. The influence of cultural expectations on the performance of individuals is hard to discount, but it is still a possibility that these expectations are, in turn, amplifying innate differences that originally accounted for the occurrence of these cultural expectations.

Clearly, within the literature on sex differences in intellectual abilities there is still much uncertainty. The differences that have been suggested could have some effect on examination performance in different subjects although, as has been pointed out by Kelly (1975), Saraga (1975), and others, there are considerable problems in attempting to relate specific intellectual abilities to achievement in specific subject areas. Also, it must be remembered that sex differences in intellectual abilities can just as easily be the result of sex-role stereotyping as can sex differences in examination performance, and they therefore cannot be assumed to reflect inherent biological differences between the sexes even if these do exist.

One must, therefore, reject any simple theory of innate sex differences in ability that might be used to account for sex differences in examination performance. The evidence for such a theory is extremely weak and, as in so many areas of psychology, it is a virtual impossibility to separate out completely the innate from the acquired.

Sex differences in attitudes towards examinations in different subjects

There would seem to be considerable consistency in studies reporting parallel sex differences in both attitudes and achievement in those subjects that are traditionally thought of as being more appropriate to one sex or the other (Ormerod 1971; 1975; Hilton and Berglund 1974; and Gardner 1975).

Hilton and Berglund's study is a particularly interesting one, in that it showed that before fifth grade in some American schools there was no difference in the Mathematics achievement scores of boys and girls, nor was there any real difference in their attitude towards Mathematics. However, from that stage on the boys moved steadily ahead of the girls both in terms of their attitude towards the subject and in terms of their achievement in it. Here again is the difficult problem of determining causation, but Hilton and Berglund concluded that it was most likely from their evidence that sex-role stereotyping was producing the difference in attitude and it was this that was, in turn, causing the difference in achievement.

Carey (1958) provides some positive evidence for the idea that less favourable attitudes towards a task can, in themselves, produce low achievement. She was working with certain problem-solving tasks, in a situation where higher male achievement appeared to be related to more positive attitudes towards these problems. She found that group discussions that were designed to produce more favourable attitudes towards these problems significantly improved female performance on them but not male performance. This result suggests that, in this case, the females

163

were not doing as well as they might have been on the task because of their poor attitude and that this situation could be changed by improving their attitude.

If this effect of attitudes on achievement is a general one, and sex-role stereotypes produce sex differences in attitudes towards different school subjects, then it is easy to see how these sex-role oriented attitudes could produce sex differences in examination performance. Further evidence, which tends to support the view that different attitudes to subjects are produced by socio-cultural influences rather than inherent differences in ability, is to be found in the work of Keeves (1973). Keeves did a cross-cultural study of sex differences in attitude and attainment in different subjects. He showed that these sex differences varied considerably between different cultures, to the extent that he concluded that the main cause of them was most likely to be found within the influence of the individual cultures. This finding has been further substantiated by the work of Kelly (1978), who studied sex differences in science achievement in fourteen countries. She found, for example, that in Japan, where sciences are part of the university entrance examinations, girls do particularly well in them. Thus, it could be proposed that each culture has its own sex-role stereotypes, which provide expectations of educational interest and success in different subjects. These ascribe different educational roles to males and females, who in turn reflect their conformity to these stereotypes through their attitudes and their examination performances in the different subjects.

Can the examination cause the difference?

People who set examinations can hardly be held responsible for sex differences in the ability of candidates, or indeed for the attitude that candidates of either sex have to the examination. It is, however, possible that an examination can be set that contains a bias towards one sex or the other.

For instance, Graf and Riddell (1972) have shown that the same problem set in two different contexts can produce quite different sex differences in performance. They set the same mathematical problem in contexts appropriate to both a female role and a male role. In one case the problem involved working out the cost of buying the right amount of lace and satin to make a dress, and in the other case a stockbroker was charging different rates of commission for buying and selling stocks for his clients. Mathematically the problem to be solved in both cases was identical, but between two controlled groups of subjects there was a marked disparity between the performance of males and females when the problem was set in the stockbroker context. This result indicated that the females found the problem much harder when it was set in the stockbroker context, and this was confirmed by comparing the 'perceived difficulty ratings' (measured on a Likert-type scale) of the groups of subjects.

The extent to which sex bias can be built into educational tests does not depend solely on problem context. Dwyer (1976) showed how a test of mathematical ability (the Scholastic Aptitude Test – Mathematics) became biased towards relatively better male performance by the inclusion of more geometry problems (requiring spatial ability) than algebra problems.

Another example of the way in which an examination may be sex biased is when a different form of assessment is used. It has frequently been observed, for instance, that when objective tests (i.e. tests made up entirely of multiple-choice questions) are introduced in place of other forms of examination, this tends to produce relatively better male performance. (This has been reported, for instance, by Wood 1978, and Murphy 1978.) Whether this is because this type of test does not test verbal ability in the way that other examinations do, or whether it is because objective tests are partly a test of the ability to break set or convergent thinking is not clear. Another possibility is that the attitude of females to objective tests is low, and this may be because they are perceived as a masculine type of activity.

On the whole, then, it does not seem as though examinations themselves are very often the cause of large sex differences in performance, although an element of sex bias is a possibility.

Efforts are taken to ensure that examinations are set so as to be fair tests for both males and females but, as we have said previously, examiners cannot be held responsible for the powerful effect that sex-role stereotyping may have in producing sex differences in examination performance. However, as Wood (1978) quite rightly points out, it is important that all examiners should be aware of these issues so that when they construct syllabuses and examinations they can seek to minimise sex bias within them.

Conclusions

Overall, it would seem to be fairly clear that sex-role stereotyping has a considerable influence within education, and in turn affects the performance of candidates of both sexes in examinations. The extent to which these stereotypes are built on actual differences in ability and the extent to which they are created by society remains unresolved, although it seems likely that the socio-cultural influence plays the bigger part.

Acknowledgement

This paper, originally presented at the BPS International Conference on Sex-Role Stereotyping, has also been published in *Educational Review* (1978) 30: 259-63.

References

BEE, H. L. (1974) Sex Differences. In H. L. Bee (ed.), *Social Issues in Developmental Psychology*. New York: Harper and Row.

BLOCK, J. H. (1976) Debatable Conclusions About Sex Differences. *Contemporary Psychology* 21:517-22.

CAREY, G. L. (1958) Sex Differences in Problem Solving Performance as a Function of Attitude Difference. *Journal of Abnormal and Social Psychology* 56:256-60.

DWYER, C. A. (1976) Test Content in Mathematics and Science: The Consideration of Sex. Paper presented at the Annual Meeting of the American Educational Research Association, San Francisco.

FAIRWEATHER, H. (1976) Sex differences in cognition. *Cognition* 4:231-80.

GARDNER, P. L. (1975) Attitudes to Science: A Review. *Studies in Science Education* 2:1-41.

GLICKMAN, J. R. (1976) Sex Differences in Intellectual Functioning: Myth or Reality. Paper presented at the Annual Meeting of the International Reading Association, Anaheim, California.

GRAF, R. G. and RIDDELL, J. C. (1972) Sex Differences in Problem-Solving as a Function of Problem Context. *Journal of Educational Research* 65:451-52.

HILTON, T. L. and BERGLUND, G. W. (1974) Sex differences in mathematics achievement – a longitudinal study. *Journal of Educational Research* 67:231-37.

HUTT, C. (1974) Sex: what's the difference? *New Scientist* (16 May).

KEEVES, J. (1973) Differences between the sexes in Mathematics and Science courses. *International Review of Education* 19:47-62.

KELLY, A. (1975) *A Discouraging Process: How Women Are Eased Out of Science*. Paper presented at the Girls and Science Education Conference, Chelsea College.

—— (1978) *Girls and Science: An International Study of Sex Differences in School Science Achievement*. Stockholm: Almquist and Wiksell.

MACCOBY, E. E. and JACKLIN, C. N. (1975) *The Psychology of Sex Differences*. London: Oxford University Press.

MONDAY, L. A., HOUT, D. P., and LUTZ, S. W. (1967) *College Student Profiles: American College Testing Programme*. Iowa City, Iowa: ACT Publications.

MURPHY, R. J. L. (1978) Sex Differences in Objective Test Performance (Unpublished Associated Examining Board Research Report).

ORMEROD, M. B. (1971) The social implications factor in attitudes to science. *British Journal of Educational Psychology* 41:335-38.

—— (1975) Science Education, Attitudes, Subject Preference and Choice. Paper presented at the Girls and Science Education Conference, Chelsea College, London.

SARAGA, E. (1975) Girls and Boys: Are there differences in ability? Paper presented at the Girls and Science Education Conference, Chelsea College, London.

WOOD, R. (1978) Sex differences in answers to English Language comprehension items. *Educational Studies* 4:157-65.

167

TEN

What sex is science?

HELEN WEINREICH-HASTE

It should surprise no-one to discover that science is perceived as 'masculine'. The popular image of the scientist is a white-coated man. This representation appears in school textbooks, in media, drama, and whenever advertisers require a 'scientific' endorsement of a product. However, the image of science has recently come under scrutiny, and it is clear that the masculinity of science is just one of a constellation of beliefs about science that constitute a mythical, storybook picture. Several writers have argued that this myth does a disservice to the understanding of scientific activity and scientific development, and may have deleterious effects on the recruitment of scientists of either sex. This paper reports a small study of some of these beliefs.

The problem

In the field of professional science, men do outnumber women.

168

The process of self-selection, towards or away from science, begins early in school. Throughout school and university, the ratio of male to female increases.

Table 10(1) *Some figures indicating the distribution of men and women in science and technology.*

		Boys %	Girls %
'A' level passes, 1972			
Maths, Physics, and Chemistry		44	16
Other sciences and Technology		10	7

		Men %	Women %
University students, subjects studied 1972-3			
Undergraduate:			
Engineering and Technology		21.8	1.4
Science		26.8	21.1
Postgraduate:			
Engineering and Technology		17.6	2.3
Science		28.0	13.9

	Ages	Men %	Women %
Employment, 1971 – skilled manpower			
Technology	18–24	32.3	0.9
	30–39	34.2	0.2
	50–59	25.7	0.1
Science	18–24	18.2	7.5
	30–39	11.4	5.6
	50–59	7.1	2.8

Source : Social Trends 1974

In *numerical* terms, therefore, science is a more male occupation than a female one. But a predominance of males and a stereotype of masculinity are not necessarily the same thing. There are a number of occupations that are predominantly the province of one sex, yet the main activity of which is stereotypically associated with the other sex: tailoring is one example, another is electronics assembly work. The stereotypic masculin-ity of science owes more to the cultural values that surround science and technology than to the presence or absence of women in their ranks. However, the sex ratio that exists in science is more likely to endorse than contradict the image.

The actual effect of stereotypes is difficult to assess. However, two predictions can reasonably be made. The first is that stereotypic masculinity is likely to act as a deterrent to girls developing an interest in science, and as an incentive to boys. The second is that the image of the 'scientific' male is likely to have an effect on the kinds of trait that the budding young male scientist aspires to possess. 'I want to be a scientist' means a great deal more than wanting to engage in scientific activity; it implies a whole lifestyle and ways of dealing with both thought and feeling.

The first prediction is borne out by a number of studies. Torr-ance (1962), for example, found a resistance among girls to tackl-ing scientific exercises. He also found that boys were better than girls at tasks involving scientific toys. 'The experimenters fre-quently heard the comment: "I'm a girl. I'm not supposed to know anything about science." ' (1963:217). The second predic-tion is also borne out, if somewhat indirectly, by studies by Mitroff of Apollo scientists (1974; et al. 1977). Mitroff found that scientists made a clear distinction between the stereotypical (in their terms, 'hypothetical') scientist and actual scientist.

This type of evidence generally supports the argument that the small numbers of women in science are a consequence of an attitude, rather than an aptitude, restriction. Certainly biologi-cal or genetic differences between the sexes could not be an adequate explanation. Some sex differences have been identified in aspects of intellectual functioning that conceivably may play some part in scientific ability, namely in spatial and mathemati-cal skills. However the differences in representation of males and females in science are far greater than could be accounted for by these differences (Maccoby and Jacklin 1975; Fairweather 1976). Furthermore, cross-cultural evidence indicates considerable var-iation in the ratio of men to women in science. Kelly (1978a; 1978b) analysed some international data on science achievement among school children. Although boys do better than girls consis-tently within each country, there was a great deal of variation in the size of the gap between them. Furthermore, girls in some

170

countries did better than boys in other countries; Hungarian and Japanese girls, for example, are better at science than boys in several Western European countries.

A number of other hypotheses have been put forward to account for the discrepancy between male and female involvement in science. Essentially, these hypotheses concern the ways in which the attitude restrictions operate, directly and indirectly. One hypothesis is that parents and teachers socialize children into appropriate sex-role behaviours, attitudes, and skills, and that this limits the chance of girls acquiring the prerequisite skills for scientific activity. A second hypothesis is that cultural expectations, which the growing individual picks up in several ways, affect the motivation of the individual, and the kinds of value, anxiety, and aspiration that indirectly affect choices such as that of career. A third hypothesis is that the gatekeepers of the scientific professions effectively discriminate against women.

The first hypothesis is only tenuously supported. On balance, it would appear that parents do not overtly treat their sons and daughters very differently, but they do transmit the cultural expectations of what it is to be male or female, and also transmit anxiety about gender role and about 'appropriate' behaviour. Thus, the little girl is not prevented or deterred from learning proto-scientific skills, but neither is she *expected* to acquire them. She also learns that she is expected to be people-oriented, which the stereotype of science does not include.

The effect of cultural expectations on personal motivation is complex. One relevant area that has been investigated extensively is the motivation to succeed, a necessary quality in the competitive field of science. The socialization of the motive to succeed is not differentiated into whether the achievement is in arts or science. Yet, while more boys than girls reach their full academic or professional potential, *many* more boys than girls reach their full scientific potential.

The stereotypes of what is sex appropriate would actually predict even less success among women than is found. Studies of stereotyping demonstrate that *both* sexes regard women as less likely than men to be competent, especially in stereotypically masculine fields. When women are presented in stimulus material as succeeding, the tendency is to attribute this to luck, or extra effort, whereas male success is attributed to ability. Con-

171

versely, failure on the part of men is attributed to luck, failure on the part of women to lack of ability (Tresemer 1974; Weinreich-Haste 1978). A large number of studies has been undertaken to establish whether women develop a motive to avoid success, as Horner contended (1970; 1972). This motive arises from the conflict between stereotypical femininity and success. While the results are somewhat inconclusive overall, it is apparent that there is anxiety about success in sex-inappropriate fields of endeavour, and in cross-sex competition, among a significant proportion of those studied.

Stereotyped thinking about sex roles and the appropriateness of certain types of behaviour depends on the individual's value system. Alper (1973) found that women who held non-traditional attitudes about sex roles were, not surprisingly, less likely to express sex stereotypes. She presented students with a picture of two white-coated women in a laboratory. The students who held traditional attitudes perceived these women as being assistants to a male scientist, temporarily absent from the laboratory. Alternatively, they described the women as being engaged in female-centred research, for example in cosmetics or perfume. The non-traditional students perceived the women as being scientists in their own right, on the brink of an exciting discovery.

The third hypothesis, that women are discriminated against in science, is difficult to test effectively in quantitative terms. Science is undoubtedly a male world, in which masculine values and lifestyles are the norm. Roe (1966) found extensive negative attitudes towards women graduate students among eminent research scientists. The anomalous woman is therefore subject to whatever pressures her male colleagues and superiors put upon her, depending on their particular reaction to her anomaly. Mitroff reports a variety of negative reactions that women scientists have encountered (*et al*. 1977). The uneasy relationship between Rosalind Franklyn and Crick and Watson is described from the men's point of view in Watson's *Double Helix* (1969). These and other accounts are inevitably anecdotal, even though consistent. However, these women are successful, they have made a career in science; while their experiences are an indication of prevailing attitudes, it is difficult to quantify the processes by which these attitudes are translated into discrimination against *potential* women scientists.

172

The study

The accumulated research suggests that the stereotypes of masculinity and femininity are quite complex. If science is perceived as masculine, it has been hypothesized that there is more to this than just a matter of a predominance of males in the profession. I carried out a study with undergraduates at the University of Bath, to try to establish the parameters of the science stereotype. There were 150 subjects, half of whom were drawn from a psychology class, the other half from the rest of the student population, predominantly science and technology students. There were equal numbers of men and women.

The subjects were asked to fill in scales, rating each of fifteen disciplines (see *Table 10(2)*). Thirteen of the disciplines were academic, two were practical. There were no differences between the ratings of male and female subjects, nor between social science and other students, so analysis was performed on the overall results.

Table 10(2) *Disciplines and rating scales*

Disciplines	Rating scales
English Literature	Hard–soft
Music	Masculine–feminine
Modern Languages	Science–arts
History	Complex–simple
Philosophy	Abstract–concrete
Cooking	Practical–theoretical
Sociology	Intellect-based – feeling-based
Political Science	
Psychology	
Economics	
Maths	
Medicine	
Biology	
Engineering	
Physics	

The scales on the whole proved to be effective as discriminators, although few disciplines were perceived as either simple or feeling-based. There emerged very defined clusters, and the intercorrelations were high (see *Table 10(3)*). In particular, there was a cluster of 'masculine' disciplines, and a cluster of 'science' disciplines. These two clusters overlapped to a very marked degree (see *Figure 10(1)*). In contrast, neither 'feminine' nor 'arts' disciplines formed a marked cluster. Therefore, when there is a significant correlation, it is possible to say with some certainty that the implications are for masculine and science disciplines; no such clarity is evident with regard to feminine and arts disciplines. After standardization of the scores, this becomes even more apparent; 'feminine' is effectively a relative concept, which might be better interpreted as 'less masculine', or 'more neuter'. 'Masculine' survives as a strong construct. The conclusion most appropriate is that, while there is 'masculine' knowledge, there is no such thing as 'feminine' knowledge, only neuter knowledge.

Table 10(3) *Intercorrelations between ratings†*

	Hard	Science	Masculine	Intellect-based	Complex	Abstract
Science	0.75*					
Masculine	0.88*	0.58				
Intellect-based	0.88*	0.85*	0.71*			
Complex	0.85*	0.88*	0.66*	0.56		
Abstract	−0.28	−0.41	−0.17	−0.39	0.05	
Practical	0.04	0.31	0.04	0.07	−0.15	−0.64*

†   Pearson product-moment correlation.
*   Significant at 1 per cent level.

The correlations with the masculine-feminine continuum indicate that 'masculine' is commensurate with *hard*, *complex*, *intellect-based*, and *scientific*. 'Science' is commensurate with *masculine*, *hard*, *complex*, *intellect-based*, *concrete*, and, to a small degree, *practical*.

174

Figure 10(1)

```
                            Arts                          6.0
                   Eng Lit  ▮
                   Music    ▮
                                                          5.0
         Mod Lang  Hist     ▮
                            ▮         Phil
         Cook               ▮
                            ▮                             4.0
            Soc             ▮
                            ▮
Feminine ── ── ── ── ── ── ──┼── ── ── ── ── ──Masculine  3.5
                            ▮         Pol sci
                            ▮
                   Psy      ▮         Eco
                            ▮                             3.0
                            ▮
                            ▮
                            ▮         Maths               2.0
                   Bio  ▮        Med
                            ▮                      Eng
                            ▮         Phys               1.0
                          Science
  6.0      5.0      4.0    3.5    3.0      2.0      1.0
```

While these results are particularly relevant to perceptions of science, they have relevance to the perception of knowledge in general also. On the whole, the dimensions are descriptive, or evocative, rather than evaluative. However a case can be made that, in the context of knowledge, 'hard-soft' has evaluative connotations. This dimension correlates highly with *science, masculine, intellect-based,* and *complex.* If we accept the evaluative nature of 'hardness' and 'softness', the implications are that non-masculine knowledge has pejorative associations.

Inspection of the results suggests that there is a halo effect, possibly arising from these evaluations. In everyday terms, it would be predicted that mathematics would be relatively neuter. Quite a high proportion of female students study mathematics, and the activity involved is, in common-sense terms, neither arts nor science. Yet mathematics is seen as highly masculine, very scientific, and *less* abstract than the social sciences. Engineering, by all conventional criteria a straightforward, practical subject, is perceived as more complex than any non-science discipline

175

except philosophy. Physics, surely an abstract subject to the laymen, is seen as more *concrete* than any arts or social science, and even more concrete than *cooking*.

It would appear that science is not only masculine; it also has an image corresponding to the cultural connotations of 'masculinity' in general. Disciplines perceived as being scientific and, therefore, masculine seem to be distorted on other continuums that have associations with the cultural stereotype of masculinity.

Some implications and conclusions

There are several possible implications of these findings. In view of the power and consistency of the stereotypic image of science, it would seem that educational programmes designed to encourage girls to do more science (or more girls to do science) are likely to encounter a number of problems. Suggestions have been made for making scientific subjects more oriented to feminine interests, and for making science more concerned with people and humanistic. While these are desirable goals in their own right, which may indeed have an effect in the classroom, the results of the study suggest that the problem is more broad. It is not only the stereotype of science that requires modification, but the stereotype of femininity, especially in relation to knowledge. Biology, for example, is an interesting exception. It is a science that is regarded as relatively feminine, and is perceived as neither hard nor soft. Yet it carries the scientific/masculine connotations of being intellect-based and concrete. It is difficult to work out why biology, particularly in contrast with, say, medicine, has these connotations. The argument that biology is studied by more girls than other sciences is circular, and, in any case, both maths and medicine have a fair proportion of female students and practitioners.

The relativism of feminine as opposed to masculine knowledge was discussed earlier. There is only one academic discipline that is clearly feminine as opposed to neuter. This is modern languages. In contrast, there are three masculine disciplines, engineering, physics, and mathematics. The argument therefore is that there is no such thing as feminine knowledge, only that some forms of knowledge are less masculine than others. For this

176

reason, 'feminizing' science is only part of the question. Knowledge perhaps needs desexing rather than feminizing. A further confounding element in the issue is that, even in 'feminine' fields of knowledge, prestige and power are associated with males. It is still not uncommon to find a predominantly female body of arts undergraduates being taught by an entirely male faculty. It has frequently been pointed out that prestige is associated with areas dominated by male practitioners (Touhey 1974; Feather 1975). The long-term aims of increasing women's participation in science must surely have an additional goal, namely to enrich and desex science without reducing its prestige.

If such strong stereotypes exist, and have some relevance to motivation and to career choice, it becomes interesting to ask how some people escaped the message, or learned to resist the stereotype. Alper's study, cited above, suggests that attitudes towards sex roles may be relevant: non-traditional sex-role attitudes are associated with less sexing of science. Some of the many studies of 'fear of success' among women students find a similar relationship between fulfilment of potential and lack of traditional sex-role attitudes. Having a working, or work-oriented, mother as a role model seems important for professional success in women (Hoffman 1972). This itself generates non-traditional sex-role attitudes (Stoloff 1973; Stewart and Winter 1974).

There have been remarkably few studies of women scientists, or of gifted women generally. In one such study, Helson (1966, 1967) found that women mathematicians were serious, highly intelligent, introverted, and independent-minded. More recently, Bachtold and Werner (1970) found that successful women psychologists had similar characteristics to Helson's sample, but additionally were more dominant, self-sufficient, and emotionally stable than a matched group of women. These characteristics are similar to those of academic men, and particularly scientists (Roe 1961), but the women were more intelligent and more unconventional.

The limited data available can do no more than confirm the picture that women, to succeed in science especially, but even to succeed in the less 'masculine' preserve of social science, need to have the personality characteristics to equip them to resist the stereotypes – and to be rather good. However, the data do not

177

make it possible to separate success from choice of science as a career. Existing evidence confounds these two variables.

The final question concerns the relationship between the stereotype and 'reality'. To what extent do the stereotypes of the scientist reflect a distortion or exaggeration of basically accurate characterization, and to what extent is the stereotype inaccurate even to the point of being detrimental? A study by Mead and Métraux (1957), with a very large sample of American schoolchildren, picked up the contrasting but not inconsistent positive and negative images of the scientist; on the one hand, scruffy, remote, and surrounded by laboratory impedimenta, on the other, brilliant, dedicated, and detached, ultimately producing or discovering something of immense value to mankind. More sophisticated versions of the same image were elicited in studies by Beardslee and O'Dowd (1961) and Bendig and Hountras (1958) with college students. A recent study by the author indicates that contemporary schoolchildren in Britain hold images very similar to those of twenty years ago (Weinreich-Haste 1979).

A number of recent writers have criticized the 'storybook myth' of the scientist. Mahoney (1976) in particular attacks the myth of the dispassionate, brilliant, logical, open-minded scientist, unbiased by emotion and motivated only by the pursuit of truth. The scientists he studied were as temperamental, biased, and motivated by the desire for personal credit as any other group of creative people.

Mitroff (1974) goes further in his critique. He studied that most élite group of scientists, so idealized by young males (especially), the Apollo scientists. In this he questioned the reality and the desirability of attributes that are stereotypically 'masculine' in the activity of science. He found that the *personality* characteristics associated with traditional masculinity were regarded by the Apollo scientists as desirable, and useful for scientists, but the traditionally masculine ways of thinking, cognitive style, and handling of emotion were *inappropriate*. As Mitroff points out, success in a male world requires possession of the qualities with which that world competes. In other words, scientists are probably no different from other successful men (and women). Mitroff's sample of scientists was particularly high in stereotypical masculine (verbal) aggression. But they and he rejected the stereotypical masculine values in the area most specifically concerned with science. Science, it would appear, needs intuition, speculation, bias (in the sense of commitment), and so forth. From the evidence of both Mahoney and Mitroff, 'real' scientists possess plenty of these qualities.

From all these sources of data, it would appear that the conclusion is that science is masquerading under a stereotype of masculinity. It seems that creative male scientists get to the top by the expression of their 'masculine' personalities, but their creativity comes from a non-masculine way of thinking. However, the schoolchild making her choice of discipline is influenced by the personality stereotype, whether positive or negative. It was earlier argued that there is a strong case for emphasizing the human side of a science, and for recognizing more widely the role that science plays in the lives of both sexes. However the reason for doing this is not simply in some way to 'feminize' science, to 'make it OK for girls'. Knowledge needs *desexing*. This should not, in fact, require a change in the nature of knowledge, merely a greater awareness of what knowledge in reality *is*, and what the processes of science (and other forms of knowledge) actually are. Whether the straightforward truth is adequate to overcome stereotypes, however, is more problematic.

Acknowledgements

The author would like to acknowledge the importance of discussions with Alison Kelly, of the University of Manchester, in the development of this paper.

References

ALPER, T. G. (1973) The relationship between role orientation and achievement motivation in college women. *Journal of Personality* 41:9-31.

BACHTOLD, L. M. and WERNER, E. C. (1970) Personality profiles of gifted women: Psychologists. *American Psychologist* 23:234-43.

BEARDSLEE, D. C. and O'DOWD, D. D. (1961) The college student image of the scientist. *Science* 133:997-1001.

BENDIG, A. W. and HOUNTRAS, P. T. (1958) College student stereotypes of the personality traits of research scientists. *Journal of Educational Psychology* 49:309-14.

CENTRAL STATISTICAL OFFICE (1974) *Social Trends 1974*. London: HMSO.

FAIRWEATHER, H. (1976) Sex differences in cognition. *Cognition* 4:231-80.

179

FEATHER, N.T. (1975) Positive and negative reactions to male an female success and failure in relation to the perceived status and sex-typed appropriateness of occupation. *Journal of Personality and Social Psychology* **31**:536-48.

HELSON R. (1966) Personality of women with imaginative and artistic interests: the role of masculinity, originality and other characteristics. *Journal of Personality* **34**:1-25.

—— (1967) Personality characterization and developmental history of creative college women. *Genetic Psychology Monographs* **76**:205-56.

HOFFMAN, L.W. (1972) Early childhood experiences and women's achievement motives. *Journal of Social Issues* **28**:129-56.

HORNER, M.S. (1970) Femininity and successful achievement: a basic inconsistency. In J. M. Bardwick, El Douvan, M. S. Horner, and D. Gutman, *Feminine Personality and Conflict*. Belmont, Calif.: Brooks/Cole.

—— (1972) Towards an understanding of achievement-related conflicts in women. *Journal of Social Issues* **28**:157-75.

KELLY, A. (1978a) *Girls and Science: an international study of sex differences in school science achievement*. Stockholm: Almquist and Wiksell.

—— (1978b) Sex differences in science achievement: an international study. Paper presented at IX World Congress of Sociology, Uppsala.

—— (ed.) (in press) *Girls and Science Education*. Manchester: Manchester University Press.

MACCOBY, E.E. and JACKLIN, C.N. (1975) *The Psychology of Sex Differences*. London: Oxford University Press.

MAHONEY, M.J. (1976) *The Scientist as Subject: the Psychological Imperative*. Cambridge, Mass.: Ballinger.

MEAD, M and MÉTRAUX, R. (1957) Image of the scientist among high-school students. *Science* **126**:384-490.

MITROFF, I.I. (1974) *The Subjective Side of Science: a philosophical inquiry into the psychology of the Apollo Moon Scientists*. New York: Elsevier Scientific Publishing Co.

MITROFF, I.I., JACOB, T., and MOORE, E.T. (1977) On the shoulders of the spouses of scientists. *Social Studies of Science* **7**:303-27.

ROE, A. (1961) The psychology of the scientist. *Science* **134**:456-59.

—— (1966) Women in science. *Personnel and Guidance Journal* **44**:784-88.

STEWART, A.J. and WINTER, D.G. (1974) Self-definition and social definition in women. *Journal of Personality* **42**:238-59.

STOLOFF, C. (1973) Who joins Women's Liberation? *Psychiatry* **36**:325-40.

TORRANCE, E.P. (1962) *Guiding Creative Talent*. Englewood Cliffs, NJ: Prentice-Hall.

TOUHEY, J.C. (1974) Effects of additional men on prestige and desirability of occupations typically performed by women. *Journal of Applied Social Psychology* **4**:330-35.

180

TRESEMER, D. (1974) Fear of success: popular but unproven. *Psychology Today* **7**:82-5.

WATSON, J. (1969) *The Double Helix*. London: Weidenfeld and Nicholson.

WEINREICH-HASTE, H.E. (1978) Sex differences in 'fear of success' among British students. *British Journal of Social and Clinical Psychology* **17**:37-42.

—— (1979). The image of science. In, A. Kelly (ed.), *Girls and Science Education*. Manchester: Manchester University Press.

PART FIVE

Androgyny

ELEVEN

Sex roles and creativity

DAVID J. HARGREAVES

Any attempt to study the relationship between sex roles and creative achievement is likely to be a hazardous undertaking at a time when the increasing acceptance of feminist ideals is changing the degree and possibly the very nature of psychological sex differences. Although men have dominated many fields of creative activity in the past, such as musical composition, painting, and natural science, there are obvious exceptions, such as literature. It would be impossible to attempt a comprehensive explanation of observed sex differences in real-life creativity within the confines of a single discipline such as psychology; one would clearly need to call upon the disciplines of biology, sociology, and anthropology at the very least. In this chapter I shall stay within the limits of psychology, and see how far experimental studies can go in tackling the question of the psychological origins of creative activity. I shall start with a brief account of the way in which psychologists have approached the fields of 'sex differences' and 'creativity', and go on to outline some empirical research that attempts to extend the scope of current approaches.

Psychological studies of sex differences and creativity

The present volume is just part of the massive explosion of research on sex differences and sex roles that has occurred in the last twenty years or so. Whereas sex-difference analyses were previously run as a subsidiary to the main theme of most empirical studies, they have now emerged as a topic of interest in their own right. The most recent comprehensive review of the field is that of Maccoby and Jacklin (1975). They assembled a large collection of studies from the major books and journals in which psychological sex differences were likely to be investigated, and made systematic comparisons between them. The criticisms that have been levelled against Maccoby and Jacklin's conclusions by workers such as Block (1976), as well as Fairweather's (1976) devastating review, tell us more about the nature of this field of investigation than about any systematic bias on the part of individual researchers. 'Sex differences' is a huge, sprawling field of a rapidly changing nature, in which experimental techniques vary widely. It is hardly surprising that clear-cut psychological sex differences do not emerge from studies that use a wide range of experimental subjects, measuring instruments, and techniques of analysis.

When we turn to the field of 'creativity', it becomes immediately apparent that the problem of test validity limits the generality of many of the conclusions that might be drawn. Most research has been based on tests of divergent thinking, which have frequently been misnamed 'creativity tests'. Whilst this research has produced a certain level of agreement about the properties of divergent tests, we have little systematic evidence relating them to appropriate criteria of creativity. Most workers would agree, however, that these tests tap a range of abilities that has some variance in common with conventional IQ tests, as well as some that are unique. Divergent thinking is one of the abilities that are increasingly being emphasized in 'progressive', child-centred education, and it is likely to give some indication of what might be called 'creative potential'.

One of the most interesting areas of this research (for a comprehensive review see Wallach (1970)) has been that in which the influence of situational and contextual factors upon divergent test performance has been investigated. Wallach and Kogan (1965) sparked off these studies when they insisted that creative thinking could only properly be assessed under appropriate conditions. They rejected the conventional 'test' setting, with its emphasis on formal procedures and time limits, in favour of an informal, game-like, and individual approach to assessment. Under these conditions, they found that divergent tests were more likely to intercorrelate highly with one another, and to exhibit low correlations with IQ scores. Wallach and Kogan's pioneering work in this field gave rise to a number of studies in which different variables were systematically manipulated, and these have recently been reviewed by Hattie (1977). Whilst Hattie's survey leads him to disagree with the view that timed test-like conditions are inappropriate, it remains clear that the experimental study of situational influences provides a valuable means of studying the interaction between cognitive, social, and motivational factors in test performance. This kind of study is paralleled by those in the emerging field of social cognition, in which the interpersonal context of standard cognitive tasks such as those of Piaget is seen as increasingly important and influential (see e.g. Donaldson 1978). Kogan (1974) has drawn particular attention to the different effects of variations in the interpersonal context of divergent thinking tests upon each sex, and we shall return to this theme in our empirical studies.

The most obvious synthesis of these two areas of inquiry would be an examination of 'sex differences in creativity'; the most cursory glance at Maccoby and Jacklin's *Creativity* section confirms that the empirical evidence is equivocal. As in other fields, studies vary widely in their sampling, conditions of administration, and so on. Maccoby and Jacklin conclude that 'tests of creativity reflect the already documented difference between the sexes in verbal skills' (1975:114), i.e. that girls are generally superior on verbal tests: and Kogan agrees that 'empirical outcomes . . . indicate a modest advantage for females over males in what might be called creativity potential' (1976:108). The clear implication is that the under-representation of women in fields of creative activity does not result from any lack of 'creative potential'; we would need to look beyond the bounds of the study of intellectual ability to find a full explanation.

A more fruitful approach to the problem of sex differences in creativity might be to depart from the comparison of ability levels on psychometric tests, and to look at the *qualitative* aspects of performance. In the rest of this chapter, I shall outline some empirical studies carried out in the United Kingdom, in Leicester that have focussed upon *styles* of performance; our emphasis is on how sex roles influence the patterning of creative performance, rather than on how the sexes differ in their levels of ability.

Sex roles in divergent thinking

Our first study (Hargreaves 1977) was an exploratory attempt to identify and manipulate sex-typed response patterns on a simple graphic divergent test: *Circles* (Torrance 1962). Subjects are simply given sheets of paper with blank circles on them (20 per sheet, in our case), and invited to use as many circles as possible as the basis for different types of drawing. We administered the test to groups of ten to eleven year olds under game-like, untimed conditions and developed a scheme for their content analysis in a pilot study. In this scheme, each drawing is placed into one of the following six categories:

1 *Life:* All representations of animate beings or their parts, e.g. faces, bodies, insects, fish.
2 *Nature:* Inanimate naturally-occurring objects or their parts, e.g. planets, spiders' webs, fruit, vegetables, snow-flakes.
3 *Sport-games:* Objects used in sport and games, e.g. balls, racquets, targets, yoyos.
4 *Mechanical-scientific:* Man-made instruments and machines, e.g. aeroplanes, bicycle wheels, railway trains, dials.
5 *Domestic:* Objects typically found in the home, e.g. plates, teapots, buttons, clothes.
6 *Abstract:* Signs and symbols, e.g. letters, numbers, Venn diagrams, musical notes.

We analysed the drawings from the pilot study as well as those of our main study by looking for sex differences in each of these categories, as well as in conventional fluency and originality scores, computed according to Yamamoto's (1964) scoring manual. Whilst there were no significant differences in either of these 'overall ability' measures in either study, we found some striking differences in the content categories. Generally speaking, the main finding to emerge was that boys produced significantly more 'Mechanical-scientific' drawings than girls, and girls produced significantly more 'Domestic' drawings than boys. These results seemed to provide some degree of support for our view that differences in style were more likely to arise than those in level of performance.

The second part of our main study produced the most surprising results. We knew from Hudson's (1968) work that changes in the instructions for divergent tests could produce some remarkable 'role changes' in sixth-form schoolboys. Hudson asked his subjects to complete the well-known *Uses for Objects* test as themselves; as Robert Higgins, the conscientious, dedicated computer engineer; and as John McMice, the uninhibited, bohemian artist. He found a surprising degree of flexibility in his subjects' responses; most notable was the gusto with which convergers threw themselves into the role of McMice when invited to do so. They produced many more ingenious, witty, violent, and obscene responses – normally the province of divergers – than in the other two conditions. We extended this approach into the area of sex roles, and were concerned with children who were several years younger. We presented our subjects with sheets of squares, as a parallel form of the *Circles* test, with the instructions: 'If you're a boy, pretend you're a girl doing these drawings; if you're a girl, pretend you're a boy doing them.' The children were greatly excited by this request, though some appeared to be having difficulty in meeting it. When we looked at the results, however, it became clear that they had generally been remarkably successful in 'switching sex roles' on the test. This is illustrated in *Figure 11(1)* overleaf: in the 'Mechanical-scientific' and 'Domestic' categories, where we had found the most striking sex differences under normal (*Circles*) conditions, there were statistically significant sex differences in the opposite direction on the *Squares* version. We were led to conclude that sex-typed response styles are clearly identifiable in terms of our analysis, and that these styles are by no means unmodifiable psychological characteristics.

Figure 11(1) Mean scores for each sex in the 'Mechanical-scientific' and 'Domestic' response categories

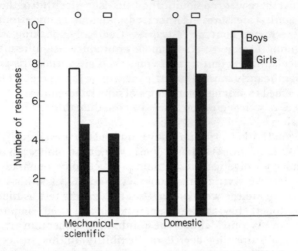

A final analysis of the same data was carried out in an attempt to push the argument further; if 'the creative man – in whatever field – tends to have more femininity in his psychological make-up than has the less creative man, and . . . the creative woman tends to possess more masculine traits than does the less creative woman' (Heim 1970:139), we predicted that subjects with high fluency scores on our *Circles* test ought to be more capable of displaying opposite-sex response styles on the *Squares* version than those with lower fluency scores. Our analysis did not confirm this prediction; in retrospect, this was hardly surprising. With ten to eleven year-old subjects, and the crude, simple measures we were using, it was rather ambitious to expect to illuminate this kind of interaction. Our first study is best regarded as a first, rough step into a complex area, and our subsequent research will employ rather more sophisticated experimental designs and procedures. We shall return to this work after a more detailed consideration of the hypothesized relationship between 'opposite-sex switching' and creativity.

'Psychological androgyny' and creativity

It is worth pausing at this stage to consider the nature and implications of the 'opposite-sex switching' that our subjects appear to be capable of. Biller (1971) has made the useful distinction between sex-role orientation, which is the individual's perception of his or her own maleness or femaleness; sex-role preference, which represents his or her own predilection for sex-typed characteristics, and sex-role adoption, which describes the behavioural outcome. Our manipulation of response styles on a cognitive test presumably operates mainly on the level of adoption, in that sex roles are consciously being enacted rather than unconsciously internalized in any sense. Biller's three components of sex roles presumably interact on our short-term test, as well as in the long-term development of the individual, and Ullian (1976) has formulated a developmental model for the evolution of conceptions of masculinity and femininity in childhood and adolescence. Urberg and Labouvie-Vief (1976) have attempted to trace this evolution into adulthood, and their 'life span developmental' perspective makes it increasingly clear that conventional notions of masculinity in males and femininity in females are inadequate and inappropriate.

This is in line with Bem's (1975) formulation of the concept of 'psychological androgyny'. Bem considers that people of both sexes should be encouraged to be 'androgynous': 'they should . . . be both instrumental *and* expressive, both assertive *and* yielding, both masculine *and* feminine – depending on the situational appropriateness of these various behaviors' (p.634). This concept enables us to develop our formulation of the relationship between the adoption of opposite-sex response styles and creativity that was touched upon in the previous section: it seems reasonable to predict that there will be a positive relationship between psychological androgyny and creativity which may hold for each sex.

Attempts that have been made in the past to test this relationship empirically have met with varying degrees of success (e.g. Barron 1957; Helson 1965; Littlejohn 1967; Biller, Singer, and Fullerton 1969; Alpaugh and Birren 1975). Perhaps the best-known research is that of MacKinnon (1962), who studied the personality characteristics of creative architects. MacKinnon's findings led him to propose that creativity is inversely related to the repression of femininity in males, and Kanner (1976) presents some recent evidence in support of this proposal. Kogan (1974), however, rejects it in favour of the view that creative males have a more balanced or diverse pattern of sex-typed interests. Kogan also considers the important question of the symmetry of the hypothesized relationship between androgyny and creativity across the sexes, and his review of the literature leads him to conclude that the evidence for increased masculinity in creative women is much weaker than that for increased femininity in creative men.

Louise Stoll and I pursued the investigation of this relationship in a follow-up to our first experiment that used a refined experimental design (Hargreaves and Stoll 1978). We went about this by assessing sex-typing with a measure that was independent from the divergent tests; this obviated the possible confounding of ideational fluency and the expression of sex roles on the tests, as well as the need to assume that *Circles* and *Squares* were parallel forms. When we looked at the literature, we soon discovered that there exists a wide and confusing variety of measures of sex-typing, many of which are inadequately standardized and validated. When Brush and Goldberg (1978) recently attempted to investigate the relationships between seven measures designed for preschoolers, they emerged with no clear-cut findings. Most measures are based on self-reports or external assessments of sex-typed games, activities, or personality characteristics; Bem's (1974) *Sex Role Inventory*, for example, requires subjects to rate themselves on twenty seven-point scales that assess masculine personality characteristics and twenty that assess feminine traits. We decided that a self-report measure of play and games activities would be most appropriate for our ten to eleven year olds, and designed our own *Play and Games Inventory* on the basis of the normative findings of Rosenberg and Sutton-Smith (1964) and Bates and Bentler (1973). It consists of a list of forty-eight play activities, twenty-two of which are normatively designated as masculine (e.g. 'football', 'playing with trains'), twenty-two as feminine (e.g. 'ballet dancing', 'playing with dolls'), and four are 'neutral' items. Children were simply asked to: 'Tick the ones you like to play'; and the number of M and F items ticked by each child was recorded.

We computed (M-F) scores for each child, and used these to divide our sample of fifty-two subjects into four groups operationally defined as 'masculine boys' (mB), 'feminine boys' (fB), 'masculine girls' (mG), and 'feminine girls' (fG). We then compared the performance of each group on two further measures:

192

Uses for Objects, administered under untimed game-like conditions, and *Circles*, this time administered under the 'opposite-sex' conditions of our first study. Our analyses of the results showed a considerable degree of support for the hypothesized relationship between androgyny and creativity. This was particularly true in the case of *Uses for Objects*: *Figure 11(2a)* shows that there is a significant interaction between sex and gender on these scores, both 'androgynous' groups (mG and fB) scoring higher than their 'non-androgynous' counterparts (mB and fG). The results from the 'opposite-sex' *Circles* test (*Figure 11(2b)* overleaf) show a similar pattern, though none of the effects are statistically significant. A striking feature of both these analyses is that it is the 'androgynous girls' (mG) who outperform the other three subject groups. This may relate to the common finding that girls of this age are less rigidly sex-typed

Figures 11(2a) and 11(2b) Mean scores of the four subjects groups on 'Uses of Objects' and 'Circles'

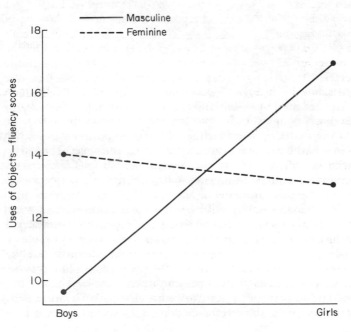

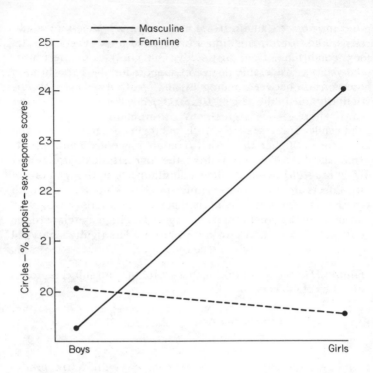

than boys (see e.g. Maccoby and Jacklin 1975). The more restricted range and standard deviation of the boys' (M-F) scores on our *Play* and *Games Inventory* seems to bear this out.

Our results suggest that the relationship between androgyny and creativity is not symmetrical across the sexes, though we must be cautious in drawing general conclusions from subject groups that are only operationally defined as 'masculine' or 'feminine' in relation to one another. The main constraint upon our approach to the problem, in fact, lies in the way in which these variables are operationalized. Self-report measures of masculinity and femininity face considerable conceptual problems (see Littlejohn 1967), and we have already pointed out that divergent test validity is one of the most pressing problems of creativity research. Although some preliminary efforts have been made in this direction (e.g. Wallach and Wing 1969), we urgently need to establish criteria for 'creativity', and these may be psychometric or non-psychometric. In the final section, I shall consider a field of study that seems to have considerable potential for the development of behavioural indices of these variables: young children's play. A preliminary outline of a pilot study we have carried out in this area will indicate the direction in which we think future research should move.

Sex roles and creativity in children's play

Lieberman (1965) was one of the first researchers to attempt a direct experimental test of the relationship between creativity and play. We have reviewed the theoretical basis for this relationship elsewhere (Hargreaves 1973); Wallach and Kogan's (1965) emphasis on the importance of playfulness in creativity confirms that the two are likely to go hand in hand. Wallach and Kogan looked for behavioural correlates of creativity in their ten to eleven year olds sample, and Hutt and Bhavnani (1972) as well as Singer and Rummo (1973) have extended this approach to the study of preschool children. It seems very likely that the sexes differ in their patterns of correlation between behavioural and cognitive styles, and that these patterns change with age. This field of study is in its infancy, however, and there are few clear-cut findings.

Our own approach was to attempt a direct behavioural analogy of the 'opposite-sex response' conditions of our previous research by observing young children's free play with toys normally associated with the opposite sex. There is a considerable body of literature in which normative sex differences in play activities have been charted (see Maccoby and Jacklin 1975); some have used naturalistic observation (e.g. Grief 1974), and some have used imitation and modelling techniques (e.g. Wolf 1975). Although studies of play with opposite-sex toys can be found in the literature (e.g. Fagot 1977), there seems to have been little direct experimental manipulation of this variable.

Peter Claydon, Anne Keane, and I attempted to do this in a pilot study of sixteen four to five year-old children (for full details see Claydon 1978). Our initial plan was to test two hypotheses: the first, which has been mentioned already, was that girls should be less rigidly sex-typed than boys in terms of their tendency to play with opposite-sex toys; second, we hypothesized that this tendency, which may be regarded as the behavioural expression of androgyny, should be positively related to divergent test scores. It proved impossible, unfortunately, to test this second hypothesis adequately because of the difficulties of assessing divergent thinking in preschoolers, and the smallness of our eventual sample. We were able, however, to gain some insight into our first hypothesis.

We invited eight boys and eight girls to visit the Psychology Department's play laboratory, along with their mothers, on two separate occasions. On each occasion the first twenty minutes was devoted to free play with a number of toys that were set out in advance, and the rest of the session (about forty minutes) to a variety of questionnaires, tests, and interviews. In the first play session, boys and girls alike were invited to play with a range of twenty-four toys; eight were normatively designated as 'masculine', eight as 'feminine', and eight as 'neutral'. In the second play session, the eight same-sex toys were removed; girls were left with 'masculine' and 'neutral' toys, and boys with 'feminine' and 'neutral' ones. All play sessions were recorded on videotape, with a supplementary verbal commentary; both of these records were then subjected to detailed analysis (see Claydon 1978).

Our first hypothesis was supported by the results from our three main measures of opposite-sex toy play: girls played with significantly more opposite-sex toys, engaged in a significantly larger number of play episodes with them, and spent a significantly greater proportion of the total time with them than did boys, in both sessions. On our fourth measure, mean attention span with opposite-sex toys, the trend was in the same direction without reaching statistical significance. Our other, more general measures showed that children of both sexes tended to move from 'exploratory' behaviour in the first session to more 'play'-like behaviour in the second, along the lines of Hutt's (1966) account. This may be confounded, however, by the simple fact that there were fewer toys available for further 'exploration' in the second session.

Perhaps the most significant outcome of this small pilot study is that it confirms the value of using behavioural indices of the variables being investigated. The research we plan for the future will pursue the relationship between androgyny and creativity in children's play as well as in pencil and paper tests; in this way, we hope to overcome at least some of the problems of test validation and the operationalization of variables that previous research has faced.

Conclusion

We have reviewed some traditional approaches to the fields of sex roles and creativity, and outlined some empirical research that emphasizes the patterning of behaviour in sex roles rather than the analysis of sex differences in levels of ability. Our results suggest that direct behavioural studies of the variables involved are likely to be most fruitful in overcoming many of the more pressing problems of pencil-and-paper research in this area.

Acknowledgement

The research reported in the section 'Sex roles and creativity in children's play' was supported by a grant from the Leicester University Research Board.

References

ALPAUGH, P.K. and BIRREN, J.F. (1975) Are there sex differences in creativity across the adult life span? *Human Development* 18:461-65.

BARRON, F. (1957) Originality in relation to personality and intellect. *Journal of Personality* 25:730-42.

BATES, J.E. and BENTLER, P.M. (1973) Play activities of normal and effeminate boys. *Developmental Psychology* 9:20-7.

BEM, S.L. (1974) The measurement of psychological androgyny. *Journal of Consulting and Clinical Psychology* 42:155-62.

——(1975) Sex role adaptability: one consequence of psychological androgyny. *Journal of Personality and Social Psychology* 31:634-43.

BILLER, H.B. (1971) *Father, Child and Sex-Role*. Lexington, Mass.: Heath Lexington Books.

BILLER, H.B., SINGER, D.L., and FULLERTON, M. (1969) Sex-role development and creative potential in kindergarten-age boys. *Developmental Psychology* 3:291-96.

BLOCK, J.H. (1976) Issues, problems, and pitfalls in assessing sex differences: a critical review of *The Psychology of Sex Differences*. *Merrill-Palmer Quarterly* 22:283-308.

BRUSH, L.R. and GOLDBERG, W.A. (1978) The intercorrelation of measures of sex-role identity. *Journal of Child Psychology and Psychiatry* 19:43-8.

197

CLAYDON, P.D. (1978) Sex typing, play and creativity in young children. Psychology Department, University of Leicester (unpublished report).

DONALDSON, M. (1978) *Children's Minds*. Glasgow: Fontana/Collins.

FAGOT, B.I. (1977) Consequences of moderate cross gender behavior in preschool children. *Child Development* 48:902-7.

FAIRWEATHER, H. (1976) Sex differences in cognition. *Cognition* 4:231-80.

GRIEF, E.B. (1974) Sex role playing in pre-school children. In, J. S. Bruner, A. Jolly, and K. Sylva (eds), *Play*. Harmondsworth: Penguin.

HARGREAVES, D.J. (1973) Creativity and Play in Children. University of Durham (unpublished Ph.D. thesis).

——(1977) Sex roles in divergent thinking. *British Journal of Educational Psychology* 47:25-32.

HARGREAVES, D.J. and STOLL, L.A. (1978) Psychological androgyny and creativity. Psychology Department, University of Leicester (unpublished report).

HATTIE, J.A. (1977) Conditions for administering creativity tests. *Psychological Bulletin* 84:1249-60.

HEIM, A.W. (1970) *Intelligence and Personality*. Harmondsworth: Pelican.

HELSON, R. (1965) Childhood interest clusters related to creativity in women. *Journal of Consulting Psychology* 29:352-67.

HUDSON, L. (1968) *Frames of Mind*. London: Methuen.

HUTT, C. (1966) Exploration and play in children. Symposia of the Zoological Society of London 18: 61–81.

HUTT, C. and BHAVNANI, R. (1972) Predictions from play. *Nature* 237:171-72.

KANNER, A.D. (1976) Femininity and masculinity: their relationship to creativity in male architects and their independence from each other. *Journal of Consulting and Clinical Psychology* 44, 802-5.

KOGAN, N. (1974) Creativity and sex differences. *Journal of Creative Behavior* 8:1-14.

——(1976) Sex differences in creativity and cognitive styles. In, S. Messick (ed.), *Individuality in Learning*. San Francisco: Jossey-Bass.

LIEBERMAN, J.N. (1965) Playfulness and divergent thinking: an investigation of their relationship at the kindergarten level. *Journal of Genetic Psychology* 107:219-24.

LITTLEJOHN, M.T. (1967) Creativity and masculinity-femininity in ninth graders. *Perceptual and Motor Skills* 25:737-43.

MACKINNON, D.W. (1962) The nature and nurture of creative talent. *American Psychologist* 17:484-95.

MACCOBY, E.E. and JACKLIN, C.N. (1975) *The Psychology of Sex Differences*. London: Oxford University Press.

ROSENBERG, B.G. and SUTTON-SMITH, B. (1964) The measurement of masculinity and femininity in children: an extension and revalidation. *Journal of Genetic Psychology* 104:259-64.

SINGER, D.L. and RUMMO, J. (1973) Ideational creativity and behavioral

198

style in kindergarten-age children. *Developmental Psychology* 8:154-61.

TORRANCE, E.P. (1962) *Guiding Creative Talent*. Englewood Cliffs, N.J.: Prentice-Hall.

ULLIAN, D.Z. (1976) The development of conceptions of masculinity and femininity. In, B. Lloyd and J. Archer (eds), *Exploring Sex Differences*. London: Academic Press.

URBERG, K.A. and LABOUVIE-VIEF, G. (1976) Conceptualizations of sex roles: a life span developmental study. *Developmental Psychology* 12:15-23.

WALLACH, M.A. (1970) Creativity. In P. H. Mussen (ed.), *Carmichael's Manual of Child Psychology*. New York: Wiley.

WALLACH, M.A. and KOGAN, N. (1965) *Modes of Thinking in Young Children*. New York: Holt, Rinehart and Winston.

WALLACH, M.A. and WING, C.W. (1969) *The Talented Student: A Validation of the Creativity-Intelligence Distinction*. New York: Holt, Rinehart and Winston.

WOLF, T.M. (1975) Response consequences to televised modeled sex-inappropriate play behavior. *Journal of Genetic Psychology* 127:35-44.

YAMAMOTO, K. (1964) *Experimental Scoring Manuals for the Minnesota Tests of Creative Thinking*. Kent, Ohio: Bureau of Educational Research, Kent State University.

TWELVE

Psychological androgyny and mental health

JENNIFER A. WILLIAMS

The study upon which I am going to report was designed to explore the relationship between sextyping and mental health in women. Confirmation was found for the main hypothesis, which was that androgynous women – those who describe themselves in terms of high levels of both male and female characteristics – would report fewer psychiatric symptoms than high masculine, high feminine, or low androgynous women. I shall introduce this study in the context of the current work on the relationship between gender role and mental disorder.

Stimulated in part by the feminist revival, several attempts in recent years have been made to collate data about the incidence of mental disorder in women (Gove 1972; Landau 1973). The findings can be briefly stated as follows:

1 Compared with men, women are significantly more likely to seek help and be treated for mental disorder, and this

applies whether the diagnosis is neurosis, psychosis, transient situational disorder, or attempted suicide;

2 That the incident rate of these disorders in women has been increasing in the last few decades.

Attempts to explain these findings in terms of the biological and hormonal aspects of being female have on the whole been inadequate (Parlee 1973; Bart 1971). There has been a similar lack of success in explaining the difference as an artefact arising from either sex-role related differences in willingness to seek help (see Clancy and Gove 1975), or to differences in the labelling process of mental illness when applied to men and women (Gove and Tudor 1973). In the main, the greatest explanatory power seems to be offered by the attempts to relate the incidence of mental illness in women to the types of social role they are expected to fulfil.

In the last ten years, several theories and a quantity of empirical research have appeared as a consequence of efforts to isolate and understand those aspects of the female role that have mental health implications. At the risk of over-simplifying, it is possible to distinguish two main approaches. The first attempts to explore the implications of the sex-role norms regarding the division of labour, i.e. what women are expected *to do*. Within this approach some of the authors have focussed on structural aspects of the roles e.g. role loss at middle age (Bart 1971; Jongeward 1972), inter-role conflict (Hall and Gardon 1973), and intra-role conflict (Fodor 1974). Others have emphasized the importance of considering the actual content of the norms (Gove and Tudor 1973; Haavio-Mannila 1976) and also the value attributed to them (Miller 1971). The mediating variables linking sex roles to mental disorder are typically regarded as being either the inherent potential of sex roles to create stress for the individual, or the effect of the roles on specific components of self-concept, in particular self-esteem. The second approach in contrast takes as its focus the implications of the sex-role norms relating to sex-appropriate personality traits, i.e. what women are expected *to be*. It is the implications of the sex differentiation of personality traits that is the main concern here.

Traditionally there has been an almost mythological belief that mental health is contingent on the successful adoption of the appropriate sex-typed personality characteristics. For example, although the biological basis of Freud's theory is largely refuted, his claim that passivity, dependence, and nurturance are healthy female attributes and that assertiveness is a sign of neuroticism would still seem to prevail among mental health professionals (Broverman *et al*. 1970; Abramovitz *et al*. 1973). Such beliefs are also found stated in a more explicit fashion in some of the major personality theories (for a review see Weisstein (1969) and Doherty (1973)). What evidence is there to support this relationship? Interpretation of the earlier literature is difficult; the problems arising from conceptualization and methodology have been discussed elsewhere (Pleck, 1975; Smith, 1977). If any conclusion can be reached, it is that whereas the adoption of sex-appropriate traits in males *is* associated with mental health, the relationship does not hold for females. High levels of femininity in women are positively associated with anxiety (Gall 1969) and negatively associated with such indices of mental health as adjustment (Rychlak and Legerski 1967; Heilbrun 1968), ego strength (Gump 1972), and autonomy (Lozoff 1972). In addition, the positive association between feminine traits and poor mental health has been found to occur even when the person is cross sex-typed (Sears 1970; Williams 1973).

While at this juncture it might seem appropriate to discuss the explanations that have been offered for these findings, it would seem rather premature given the numerous critiques that have been made of the masculinity/femininity (M/F) scales on which most of the findings are based. As well as the low correlation found between scales used (Tyler 1968), a number of writers have pointed to another major restriction (Carlson 1971; Constantinople 1973): that is, M and F have been conceptualized as opposite ends of a bipolar continuum. The possibility is therefore precluded of an individual being both M *and* F. In response to this criticism, several inventories have now been created that make it possible to calculate the extent to which an individual perceives him or herself in terms of these characteristics (Spence *et al*. 1975; Bem 1974).[2] As Bem (1974) notes, the category of people previously obscured in the earlier inventories were those who had a balance of both M and F, people she called 'androgynous'. While the concept of androgyny had been introduced into the social sciences several years earlier (Rossi 1964), it took rather longer to enter the discourse on sex-typing and mental health, although some studies anticipated it (Heilbrun 1968; Rychlak and Legerski

1967). Bem suggested that androgyny could well define a new standard of mental health given the wider repertoire of behaviour at the disposal of such people. She later demonstrated, at least within the confines of experimental conditions, that androgynous men and women were more situationally effective, that is, they were more able to engage in appropriate behaviour of both typical male and female types (Bem 1975).

In another study, Spence, Helmreich, and Stapp (1975) argue that the level of M and F should be considered as well as the balance. The argument is supported by their examination of the relationship between self-esteem and sex-typing in both men and women. The results showed that high androgynous people were the highest in self-esteem, followed by those high in masculinity, and then those high in femininity, while those who were low androgynous were lowest in self-esteem. The finding that high masculine women had higher self-esteem than high feminine women is familiar; the advantage of cross sex-typing in terms of mental health was also suggested by some of the earlier studies mentioned.

One of the major problems in extrapolating from studies in this area was that subjects were, with few exceptions (Block et al. 1973; Harford et al. 1967), limited to children, adolescents, and students. The relationships between sex-typing and mental health in these groups does not necessarily hold for the mature adult, as shown by one of the few studies on adult males by Mussen (1962). In this study even the positive association between high levels of masculinity in males and mental health was found not to occur. In addition, the consistent finding that masculine women had a higher self-esteem or better adjustment than feminine women may be contingent on the social situation of the subjects. In the androcentric world of education, the disadvantages of being cross sex-typed might be minimized and the advantages maximized. It is after formal education is completed that the full effect of the division of labour is apparent, and when most women are funnelled into traditional female roles and occupations. It seems possible that the advantage of masculine women over feminine women in terms of mental health may not then occur.

It was therefore decided to examine the relationship between mental health and sex-typing in a sample of women drawn at random from the population. Furthermore, as level of self-esteem does not have a one-to-one relationship with mental disorder or health, it was decided to look at the relationship between sex-typing and the report of psychiatric symptoms. In addition, hypotheses were tested about the way sex-typing mediates psychological health in women. We know from work on environmental stress and mental disorder that:

1 Life events or changes produce psychological distress in individuals in the general population (Dohrenwend 1961; Brown *et al*. 1973);
2 Differences in the incidence rates of mental disorder between certain social categories such as race and class can be partly attributed to category-related differences in the amount of life changes and events, and also category-related differences in vulnerability to stress (Dohrenwend 1973; Brown *et al*. 1975).

It is, therefore, suggested that the low incidence of psychiatric disorder in high androgynous women would be partly attributable, first, to low life stress because of the more effective interaction with the social environment in this group, and, second, to low vulnerability to life stress because the greater array of behaviours at the disposal of this group will increase the possibility of coping adaptively with stress. The following hypotheses were then formulated with regard to women:

I   That the high androgynous (HA) group of women would have the lowest incidence of self-reported psychiatric symptoms.

II   That there would be no difference between high masculine (HM) and high feminine (HF) groups in the psychiatric symptoms reported.

III   That the low androgynous (LA) group of women would have the highest incidence of self-reported psychiatric symptoms.

IV   That the high androgynous (HA) group would be less vulnerable to life stress, that is, least likely to respond to stress by reporting psychiatric symptoms.

V   That high androgynous (HA) women would report the least amount of life stress in the previous year.

Method

SUBJECTS

The study was carried out in 1976. A subject pool of 215 women, aged between eighteen and sixty-five years, was drawn at random from a computer-stored register of a Bristol Health Centre. Of the original sample, 68 per cent (147 women) were successfully contacted; the remainder had changed address. Of these, 73 per cent (107) returned the questionnaire completed. Three however were discarded as they were incomplete, the final sample being 104 women.

While the method of contact used is biased against the inclusion of those women who were coping with the stress of recently moving house, it was felt that this would not have any serious implications for the findings.

To determine if the women answering the questionnaire differed from women who did not, the frequency of visits to the Health Centre in the last two years was used to test for response bias. No significant difference was found between the mean number of visits for responders and non-responders (responders $\bar{x}=5.46$, non-responders $\bar{x}=6.18$; $t=0.5694$ n.s.). While this measure tells us about the representativeness of the sample in terms of physical health, psychological health is arguably also reflected (Eastwood and Trevelyan 1972).

MEASURES

The Bem Sex Role Inventory (BSRI) was used to determine the sex-typing of the subjects (Bem 1974). This instrument contains both an M and F scale each of which has twenty items selected on the basis of their desirability for either sex. Twenty filler items, neutral as regards sex, were also included. Following the median split procedure described by Spence *et al.* (1975), the four sex-typed groups were obtained.

The General Health Questionnaire (GHQ) was used to assess psychiatric symptomatology (Goldberg 1972). This requires subjects to answer fifty questions about general medical complaints and health in the past few weeks. The questionnaire is based on a model of psychiatric (non-psychotic) disturbance that varies on a dimension from hypothetical normality to severe disorder. In

205

addition, Goldberg (1972) has demonstrated the validity of the use of a cut-off point on the dimension above which (within known limits of error) it is possible to categorize people as potential 'psychiatric cases'.

The Life Events Inventory (LEI) was used to calculate the subject's life stress in the previous year (Cochrane and Robertson 1973). The LEI is a modified version of the Homes and Rahe Life Events Inventory, and consists of a check list of fifty-five life events with space for subjects to indicate which, if any, of the events have occurred in the last year. The subjects' LEI scores were calculated by summing the mean weight of each item that is marked. The life events have also been categorized on the basis of whether they could be regarded as being within the control of the subject or beyond the control of the subject (Cochrane and Robertson 1975).

With the assistance of one of the physicians, the frequency of visits to the Health Centre in the last two years was obtained from the subjects' medical records. Problems in locating some of the records resulted in these data being available for only 74 per cent (seventy-seven) of the subjects.

PROCEDURE

The questionnaires were mailed to the subjects. A standard cover note from the Health Centre was included asking for their co-operation. The subjects were told that the questionnaires should take under twenty minutes to complete and they were requested to return them within one week; those who did not received reminders.

Results and discussion

Using the median cut-off procedure, subjects were distributed in the four sex-typed groups and appear together with mean scores on the dependent measures in *Table 12(1)*.[3]

Hypothesis I was confirmed in that the HA group had the lowest mean GHQ scores (all ts sig., $p < .05$). In addition, they were also the group with the lowest number of women who could feasibly be regarded as 'psychiatric cases'. There were in fact none in this group that met Goldberg's criterion (chi-square = 6.89, df = 3, $p < .05$). They were also the group who visited the

Table 12(1) *Scores for each sex-typed category*

	HA women	HM women	HF women	LA women	All women
X̄ GHQ (Psychological disturbance score)	28.55	40.03	40.70	43.79	38.67
% 'Psychiatric cases'	0%	31%	32%	45%	27%
X̄ Visits to Health Centre in last two years	3.50	5.68	5.22	7.14	5.51
	(n = 16)	(n = 22)	(n = 18)	(n = 21)	(n = 77)
X̄ Life events in the last year	2.75	4.65	3.54	4.12	3.83
X̄ LEI (weighted life stress score for the last year)	108.40	192.72	147.70	171.54	158.59
X̄ 'Uncontrolled' life events	0.40	0.58	0.58	1.04	0.65
X̄ 'Controlled' life events	2.35	4.06	2.96	3.08	3.18
X̄ LEI score: Uncontrolled life events	11.20	23.06	21.54	51.50	26.26
X̄ LEI score: Controlled life events	97.20	169.65	126.16	120.04	132.32
Ratio uncontrolled/controlled life events	1:5.87	1:6.94	1:5.11	1:3.16	1:5.01
Ratio uncontrolled/controlled LEI scores	1:8.69	1:7.36	1:5.86	1:2.33	1:5.03

HA women = High masculine/High feminine or High androgynous (n = 20)
HM women = High masculine/Low feminine or High masculine (n = 29)
HF women = Low masculine/High feminine or High feminine (n = 31)
LA women = Low masculine/Low feminine or Low androgynous (n = 24)

Health Centre least often in the last two years (ts sig., p<.05).

Hypothesis II was also supported, no significant differences being found between the mean GHQ scores of the HM and HF groups. This adds credence to the argument that the previous-found advantage of being cross sex-typed in terms of mental health was contingent on the nature of the populations investigated.

Hypothesis III was not confirmed in that the LA group did not have significantly higher symptom scores than the other women. This was felt to be attributable to the lack of sensitivity of the scale used, an explanation supported by the fact that the LA group had the highest mean visits to the Health Centre (all ts sig., p<.05).

No support was gained for Hypothesis IV, which was that the HA women would be least likely to respond to stress by displaying psychiatric symptoms. Regression of the GHQ scores with factors M, F, and LEI gave a significant effect for life stress only (t = 2.77, p<.005). M and F were not found to be significant variables affecting vulnerability to life stress. Although no significant difference was found between the correlations of LEI and GHQ scores for each of the sex-typed groups the data do seem to indicate that some interactions of level of M and F have implications for vulnerability to life stress. While HM and HF women have similar GHQ scores, the former experienced significantly more life stress in the previous year (t = 1.70, p<.05).

The confirmation of the final Hypothesis, that HA women would have the lowest mean LEI scores (all ts sig., p<.05), did support the notion that the relationship between M and F and life stress was one way in which sex-typing affects mental health.

Further analyses showed, as expected, that both M and F had implications for the mental health of women. The GHQ scores were negatively correlated with both M and F (r = −.162, p<.05; r = −.206, p<.025 respectively). A 2 × 2 ANOVA of the GHQ scores with factors M and F, and levels high and low, gave an effect for both M and F (f = 3.96, df = 1,103, p<.05; f = 4.87, p<.05). Only F, however, was found to be significantly negatively correlated with LEI scores (r = −.22, p<.05), and a 2 × 2 ANOVA of the scores with factors M and F and levels high and low gave a significant effect for F only (f = 3.99, p<.05). Therefore, while the association between high femininity and low life stress would seem to provide at least a partial explanation for the relationship with mental health, the same argument cannot be applied to high masculinity.

One possible reason for these findings is that the effect of M was limited to only those life events *within* the control of the individual, and the inclusion of life events *outside* the control of the subject might be masking this.[4] To test this, the life events were divided into 'controlled' and 'uncontrolled', and separate analyses carried out (Cochrane and Robertson 1975). Uncontrolled life events were 17 per cent of all events, and although the frequency was low for the group, an ANOVA being impossible on these data, both M and F significantly affected their distribution (ps $<$ .05 and $<$ .04 respectively). Both high levels of M and F were associated with low frequency of these (uncontrolled) life events.

A 2×2 ANOVA on the LEI scores of the controlled life events with factors M and F and levels high and low gave a significant effect for level of F and also a significant interaction (f = 4.02 and 3.96 respectively, ps $<$ .05). As can be seen in *Table 12(1)*, while a high level of F is associated with lower stress, a high level of M is only associated with low stress in the presence of a high level of F. The outcome of this is that whereas HA women have significantly lower controlled stress than other groups (ts sig., p $<$ .05), HM women have significantly higher controlled stress than HF women (t = 1.69, p $<$ .05).

Finally comparing the means and ratio of each group for controlled and uncontrolled stress, HA women report the lowest mean stress and the highest ratio of controlled to uncontrolled stress. HM women have a higher ratio of controlled to uncontrolled stress than HF women but this is due to the higher amount of controlled stress in the HM group; there was no difference in the uncontrolled stress. LA women have the lowest ratio of controlled to uncontrolled stress.

General discussion

The results confirm the hypothesis that possession of high levels of both M and F characteristics in women is positively related to mental health. The belief that this was because high levels of each favourably affect vulnerability to life stress was not, however, supported. This was surprising given the previous-found association between sex-typing and one indicator of psychiatric

209

vulnerability, namely self-esteem (Spence *et al*. 1975). Nevertheless, HM women did appear to be less vulnerable to stress than HF women. It is suggested that this can be explained in terms of the nature of the characteristics themselves. It is possible that HM women experience greater subjective control over what happens to them and that this renders the stress less potent. That the amount of control felt over life events is important in the mediation of stress in women has been shown previously (Dohrenwend 1973). This explanation gains support from the results of a recent study I conducted in an independent sample of women, where HM women when compared with the other groups on the locus of control scale (Rotter 1966) had lower external scores, i.e. they felt more in control of their lives than the other groups (ts sig., $p < .05$).

Let us consider the finding that both high levels of M and F were negatively associated with the occurrence of life events *beyond* the control of the individual. One possible explanation is that the individual feels less personally effective and fills in the BSRI scale accordingly. However, given the stability and centrality traditionally attributed to these traits of M and F, this seems unlikely. Nevertheless, until longitudinal data are available it cannot be dismissed. More plausible is the notion that sex-typing has an effect on the selection and creation of an environment in which uncontrolled life events are likely to occur. This indirect effect on life stress is then feasibly one way in which sex-typing mediates the mental health of women.

Similarly, the finding that high F in women is associated with lower life stress arising from life events *within* the control of the individual suggests that this is how the level of F mediates the mental health of women. The effect of high M, however, only applies when women also possess high levels of feminine traits, that is, in the HA group. It can be speculated that women who possess a high level of feminine traits are likely to deal effectively with interpersonal relationships and have a passive orientation to many aspects of the environment – both these factors contributing to a reduction of stressful life events. In contrast, women who possess a high level of masculine traits are likely to have an active orientation to the environment, and also be less likely to deal effectively with interpersonal relationships – both these factors contributing to an increase of stressful life events. The possession of high levels of both M and F in the HA group lead to effectiveness in both expressive and instrumental domains and is reflected in the low life stress reported in this group.

In summary, sex-typing was found to affect the mental health of women. While the process is more complex than first envisaged, the effects of levels of M and F on the avoidance and generation of life stress in women would seem to be one way in which this is mediated. Given these findings it is clear that we need to know more about the developmental aspects of androgyny; fortunately, there is a growing interest in this (Allgeier 1975; Kelly and Worell 1976; Ryaff and Baltes 1976). In addition, it would also seem to be important to examine the effects, if any, of the various therapies on sex-role self-concept. Given the inherent problems of response bias when obtaining data by self-report, it is also evident that we need to validate these findings using other methodologies.

Notes

1 I should like to express my sincere gratitude to Andrew Treacher for his valuable advice and encouragement during the design and execution of this work, Michael Whitfield and colleagues for their co-operation and assistance, and Howard Giles for his helpful comments on previous drafts of the paper.
2 For a critique of these scales, see Smith (1977).
3 The median points for the categorization were derived from female data only. However, a re-analysis was carried out with median point derived from both male and female data collected in a later study. While the distribution of the subjects in the sex typed categories was slightly altered, that is, more women were now categorized as HF, the findings were not affected.
4 To illustrate, an example of a controlled event is 'purchasing own house', an example of an uncontrolled event 'death of spouse'.

References

ABRAMOWITZ, S.L., ABRAMOWITZ, C.V., JACKSON, C. and GOMES, B. (1973) The politics of clinical judgment: What nonliberal examiners infer about women who do not stifle themselves. *Journal of Consulting & Clinical Psychology* **41**:385-91.
ALLGEIER, E.R. (1975) Beyond sowing and growing: The relationship of sex-typing to socialization, family plans and future orientation. *Journal of Applied Psychology* **5**:217-26.
BART, P.B. (1971) Depression in middle-aged women. In, V. Gornick and K.

Moran (eds), *Women in Sexist Society*, pp. 163-86. New York: Signet.

BEM, S. (1974) The measurement of psychological androgyny. *Journal of Consulting & Clinical Psychology* **42**:155-62.

—— (1975) Sex role adaptability: One consequence of psychological androgyny. *Journal of Personality & Social Psychology* **31**:634-43.

BLOCK, J., VON DER LIPPE, A., and BLOCK, J.H. (1973) Sex role socialization patterns: Some personality concomitants and environmental antecedents. *Journal of Consulting & Clinical Psychology* **41**:321-41.

BROVERMAN, I.K., BROVERMAN, D.M., CLARKSON, F.E., ROSENKRANTZ, P.S., and VOGEL, S.R. (1970) Sex Role Stereotypes and Clinical Judgements of Mental Health. *Journal of Consulting & Clinical Psychology* **34**:1-7.

BROWN, G.W., BHROLCHÁIN, M.N., and HARRIS, T. (1975) Social class and psychiatric disturbance among women in an urban population. *Sociology* **9**:225-54.

BROWN, G.W., SKLAIR, F., HARRIS, T.O., and BIRLEY, J.L.T. (1973) Life events and psychiatric disorders. Part I: Some methodological issues. *Psychological Issues* **3**:74-87.

CARLSON, R. (1971) Sex differences in ego functioning: Exploratory studies of agency and communion. *Journal of Consulting & Clinical Psychology* **37**:267-77.

CLANCY, K. and GOVE, P. (1975) Sex differences in mental illness: An analysis of response bias in self-report. *American Journal of Sociology* **80**:205-16.

COCHRANE, R. and ROBERTSON, A. (1973) The Life Events Inventory: A measure of the relative severity of psycho-social stressors. *Journal of Psychosomatic Research* **17**:135-37.

—— (1975) Stress in the lives of parasuicides. *Social Psychiatry* **10**:161-71.

CONSTANTINOPLE, A. (1973) Masculinity-femininity: An exception to a famous dictum? *Psychological Bulletin* **80**:387-407.

COSENTINO, F. and HEILBRUN, A. B. Jr., (1964) Anxiety correlates of sex role identity in college students. *Psychological Reports* **14**:729-30.

DOHERTY, M.A. (1973) Sexual bias in personality theory. *Counselling Psychologist* **4**:67-75.

DOHRENWEND, B.P. (1961) The social psychological nature of stress: A framework for causal inquiry. *Journal of Abnormal & Social Psychology* **62**:294-302.

DOHRENWEND, B.S. (1973) Social Status and stressful life events. *Journal of Personality & Social Psychology* **28**:225-35.

EASTWOOD, M.R. and TREVELYAN, M.H. (1972) Relationship between physical and psychiatric disorder. *Psychological Medicine* **2**:363-72.

FODOR, I. (1974) Sex role conflict and symptom formation in women: Can behaviour therapy help? *Psychotherapy: Theory, Research & Practice* **11**:22-9.

GALL, M.D. (1969) The relationship between masculinity-femininity and manifest anxiety. *Journal of Clinical Psychology* **25**:294-95.

212

GOLDBERG, P. (1972) *A Technique for the Identification and Assessment of Non-Psychotic Psychiatric Illness.* London: Oxford University Press.

GOVE, W.R. (1972) The relationship between sex roles, marital status and mental illness. *Social Forces* **51**:34-44.

GOVE, W.R. and TUDOR, J.F. (1973) Adult sex roles and mental illness. *American Journal of Sociology* **78**:50-73.

GUMP, J.P. (1972) Sex role attitudes and psychological wellbeing. *Journal of Social Issues* **28**:79-92.

HAAVIO-MANNILA, E. (1976) Ecological and sex differences in the hospitalization of mental illness in Finland and Sweden. *Social Science & Medicine* **10**:77-82.

HALL, D.T. and GORDON, F.E. (1973) Career choices of married women: Effects on conflict, role behaviour and satisfaction. *Journal of Applied Psychology* **58**:42-8.

HARFORD, T.C., WILLIS, C.H., and DEABLER, H.L. (1967) Personality correlates of masculinity-femininity. *Psychological Reports* **21**:881-84.

HEILBRUN, A.B., Jr. (1968) Sex role identity in adolescent females: A theoretical paradox. *Adolescence* **3**:79-88.

JONGEWARD, D. (1972) What do you do when script runs out? *Transactional Analysis* **2**:78-80.

KELLY, J.A. and WORELL, L. (1976) Parent behaviours related to masculine, feminine, and androgynous sex role orientations. *Journal of Consulting and Clinical Psychology* **44**: 843-51.

LANDAU, B. (1973) Women and mental illness. *Ontario Psychologist* **5**:51-7.

LOZOFF, M. (1972) Changing life style and role perceptions of men and women students. Paper presented at Radcliffe Institute Conference, Women: Resources for a Changing World, Cambridge, Mass.

MILLER, J.B. (1971) Psychological consequences of sexual inequality. *American Journal of Orthopsychiatry* **41**:767-75.

MUSSEN, P.F. (1962) Long term consequences of masculinity of interests in adolescence. *Journal of Consulting & Clinical Psychology* **26**:435-40.

PARLEE, M.B. (1973) The premenstrual syndrome. *Psychological Bulletin* **80**:454-65.

PLECK, J.H. (1975) Masculinity-femininity: Current and alternative paradigms. *Sex Roles* **1**:161-78.

ROSSI, A.S. (1964) Equality between the sexes: An immodest proposal. *Daedalus* **93**: 607-52.

ROTTER, J.B. (1966) Generalized expectancies for internal versus external control of reinforcement. *Psychological Monographs* **80** (whole no. 609).

RYAFF, C.D. and BALTES, P.B. (1976) Value transition and adult development in women: The instrumentality-terminality sequence hypothesis. *Developmental Psychology* **12**:567-68.

RYCHLAK, J.F. and LEGERSKI, A.T. (1967) A sociocultural theory of approp-

213

riate sexual role identification and level of personal adjustment. *Journal of Personality* **35**:31-49.

SEARS, R.R. (1970) Relation of early socialization experiences to self-concepts and gender role in middle childhood. *Child Development* **41**:267-89.

SMITH, P.M. (1977) Talking about androgyny: Getting there is half the fun. Paper presented at International Sex Role Stereotyping Conference, UWIST, Cardiff (July).

SPENCE, J.T., HELMREICH, R. and STAPP, J. (1975) Rating of self and peers on sex role attributes and their relation to self-esteem and conceptions of masculinity and femininity. *Journal of Personality & Social Psychology* **32**:29-39.

TYLER, L. (1968) Individual differences: Sex differences. In, D. Sills (ed.), *International Encyclopaedia of the Social Sciences*, New York: Macmillan.

WEISSTEIN, N. (1969) Kinder Kuche Kirche as scientific law: Psychology constructs the female. *Motive* **29**:78-85.

WILLIAMS, J.H. (1973) Sexual role identification and personality functioning in girls: A theory revisited. *Journal of Personality* **41**:1-8.

PART SIX

Intervention strategies to reduce sex-role stereotyping in educational programmes

THIRTEEN

Intervention strategies to reduce sex-role stereotyping in education

RUTH B. EKSTROM

Several government programmes developed in the United States in the past few years have had as a goal the improvement of educational opportunities for women and the removal of barriers that limit women's participation in education. These programmes have had two main objectives:

1 Eliminating overt discrimination and providing equal educational opportunities and treatments, and
2 Eliminating covert discrimination and providing educational equity.

The elimination of overt educational discrimination and the provision of equal educational treatment for women and men has been greatly facilitated by the enactment of legislation known as Title IX of the *Education Amendments* of 1972. Title IX prohibits sex discrimination in areas such as: admissions to vocational, graduate, professional, and public undergraduate schools; access

217

to courses and programmes; counselling and guidance; physical education and athletics; vocational education programmes; student rules and policies; financial assistance; student housing; extracurricular activities; and employment in educational institutions.

The provision of equal educational opportunities and treatments is a necessary but not sufficient condition to bring about educational equity. Educational equity means that the results of the educational process are determined by individuals' abilities, aptitudes, and interests and not by age, race, sex, or other educationally irrelevant characteristics. Educational equity does not always mean equal or identical educational treatments. For example, if blind and sighted students are given the same textbooks as instructional materials, the treatment is equal but inequitable. In order to treat blind students equitably, a special treatment (such as textbooks in Braille) must be provided.

In order to provide educational equity for women it is necessary to remove the sources of covert discrimination and, sometimes, to provide special educational treatment. Both of these can be done by designing interventions that will reduce sex-role stereotyping in education. Such programmes are being carried out in the United States under legislation known as the *Women's Educational Equity Act*. This provides funds for activities such as:

1 The development and evaluation of curricula, textbooks, and other educational materials;
2 Model pre-service and in-service training programmes for educational personnel;
3 Research and development activities designed to advance educational equity;
4 Guidance and counselling activities, including the development of non-discriminatory tests;
5 Educational activities to increase opportunities for adult women; and
6 The expansion and improvement of educational programmes for women in vocational education, career education, physical education, and educational administration.

Further information about the act and the activities supported by it can be obtained from the Women's Program Staff, United States Office of Education, Washington, DC 20202, USA.

In this paper I shall describe how intervention programmes to reduce sex-role stereotyping in education can be designed and developed, using some of the projects funded under the *Women's Educational Equity Act* as examples.

Designing such a programme first involves knowing if and when sex stereotyping or covert discrimination has occurred.

Identifying sex stereotyping and covert discrimination in education

Sex stereotyping has been defined in the Rules and Regulations of the *Women's Educational Equity Act* (United States Office of Education 1976) as 'the attribution of behaviors, abilities, inter-interests, values and roles to a person or group of persons on the basis of their sex'. Sex-role stereotypes assume that because individuals share a common gender they also share interests, abilities, and values. Sex-role stereotypes are developed and perpetuated in our society by the socialization processes that take place in the home and the school as well as by various influences in the community and the media.

It is not always easy to tell when covert discrimination has taken place. As was pointed out by Ramaley in a symposium on Covert Discrimination in the Sciences, covert discrimination is 'subtle, rarely conscious, and, therefore, difficult to confront and change. It is this set of hidden assumptions about how men and women should behave and the goals that they should set for themselves that . . . alters the atmosphere in which people work and interact' (Ramaley 1978).

In schools and other educational settings, we may suspect that sex-stereotyping or covert discrimination has taken place when the outcomes of identical educational treatments are different for male and female students with the same aptitudes, abilities, and interests; or when different educational and/or career futures are suggested for females and males with the same aptitudes, abilities, and interests. A third index that covert discrimination may have occurred, suggested by Theodore (1971), is 'when females of equivalent qualification, experience and performance as males do not share equally in the decision-making process nor receive equal rewards. These rewards consist of money, promotions, prestige, professional recognition, and honors'.

In the classroom, we may be able to observe sex stereotyping

219

directly in teacher-pupil or pupil-pupil interactions. Other indirect evidence for and indicators of sex stereotyping can be observed in the classroom. These include the textbooks and other instructional materials that are used and the content of the curriculum itself. Textbooks tend to portray relatively few females and these mostly in traditional female roles such as mother, teacher, or nurse. Interest tests and guidance materials often reflect these same views by, for example, encouraging girls to become secretaries while boys with the same interests are encouraged to become business executives. Often the curriculum provides home economics training as the only vocational education for girls while boys have the option to enter a variety of technical training programmes in areas like mechanics, carpentry, etc. Similarly, physical education programmes for girls and boys may be very different in their nature and may not provide similar opportunities to develop co-ordination, stamina, and teamwork experiences. Finally, most curricula neglect almost entirely the contributions that women have made to our culture and civilization.

There are a variety of barriers, too, to women's full participation in college-level education (Ekstrom 1972). Since Title IX these rarely include institutional practices that place limits on the number of women entering college or receiving financial aid. However, the type of curriculum offered, the services that are available (and not available), and the attitudes of faculty and administrators towards women still serve as deterrents to women's entrance into and continuation in higher education.

But we can also observe sex-role stereotyping in the structure of the educational system itself. In the United States, 66 per cent of public (government-supported) school teachers are female but only 12.7 per cent of the principals (who are in charge of individual schools) are female, and among superintendents (who direct all of the schools for a city or district) less than 1 per cent are female. In our colleges, only 19 per cent of the faculty are women and, even more discouraging, except in the few remaining women's colleges, there are only a handful of women serving as college or university presidents.

Clearly interventions are needed if these practices are to be changed. We can think of creating change in education as being similar to designing other types of social technology (Morrish 1976).

practical steps

Designing an intervention programme

Before an intervention programme to create educational changes aimed at reducing sex-role stereotyping can be designed or implemented, several steps are necessary:

1 The researcher must define sex stereotyping and s/he must analyse the educational system to determine when, where, and how this stereotyping occurs and who are the individuals transmitting or causing these stereotypes.

2 The researcher must decide on the target group for intervention that will best deal with the causes of these stereotypes. In some cases, such as teacher-pupil classroom interaction, it may be possible to go directly to the sources. In other cases, e.g. textbooks, the publishers may be more difficult to reach, so it may be necessary to work indirectly by sensitizing teachers to the stereotypes in these materials and how to overcome them. It is useless to direct a programme at an inappropriate group. For example, programmes to encourage more women teachers to become school administrators may be relatively ineffective if the group making the hiring decisions (such as the local school board for public schools in the United States) still holds stereotypes about women's ability to lead and administer.

3 When the appropriate target group has been identified, the individuals involved must be made aware of the fact that they hold sex-role stereotypes. This is a very sensitive problem and is a point where anger, guilt, and resentment of the target population can make it impossible to continue the intervention programme.

4 At the same time, the designer of the programme must determine what incentives for change exist or can be devised. This is a very difficult part of an intervention programme and one that is too often overlooked by individuals who feel that the negative consequences of sex stereotyping are so obvious that anyone who is made aware of the problem should be amenable to changing their behaviour. For teachers, promotion to a new salary range or college credit can be used as incentives. However, implementing these requires the help and support of those school and government officials further up the educational hierarchy and these are, most typically, males who may themselves have little

221

awareness of the problem.

5 Only at this stage is it appropriate to introduce the actual treatment. This is typically a modelling of preferred behaviour and/or an introduction of factual data and information to correct the stereotypes.

6 However, the treatment itself cannot be considered to complete an intervention design. Evaluation of the attitude and information changes and/or monitoring of behaviour is also necessary if you are to know if the treatment is effective and if the results are lasting.

7 Finally, while it is not imperative to do so, it is highly desirable to include within the intervention some plan for further dissemination. When those who have received the treatment can serve as trainers for others or as expert resources, the final per-person cost of providing the intervention is greatly reduced.

Several books have appeared recently on the general problem of designing change in education (Eiben and Milliren 1976; Havelock 1973; Morrish 1976). From these we know that educational innovation is more readily accepted by individuals who are young, have high social status, are self-confident, and who are willing to take risks. We also know that new educational programmes are more readily accepted by individuals if they have a proven quality, are low cost, are divisible in parts or segments, are easily communicated to others, are not complex, have strong leadership, and have an effective system of rewards. It is, according to the literature, especially important that the proposed change is compatible with the values and existing practices of adopters, that the group is ready for change, and that the proposed change is acceptable to the surrounding community. These, of course, are difficult, if not near impossible, goals to achieve when dealing with sex-role stereotyping.

This is why the Federation of Organizations for Professional Women at a recent conference on Effecting Social Change for Women (1976) has stressed the great importance of dialogue and interaction between researchers and activists in producing social change. It is also the reason that many of the intervention projects that are described below are working simultaneously with parents and community groups as well as with the schools.

Examples of intervention programmes

Some examples of educational interventions to reduce sex stereotyping are drawn from current projects in the United States. The projects are funded under the *Women's Educational Equity Act* (WEEA). In 1976-7, the first year in which this programme was in effect, sixty-seven grants were made. These included large grants dealing with three priority areas:

1 Sexism in education
2 Educational leadership and
3 Career preparation.

Small grants were made for other, more general, or innovation projects. Each of these grants is developing disseminable intervention programmes and training materials that can be used widely and which will further educational equity for women.

One group of projects has been dealing with providing intervention through the pre-service or in-service training of teachers. They include the identification of sex stereotyping in the classroom, and changing behaviour to make it more equitable. Interventions with pre-service teachers are less difficult since these individuals are already in a relatively positive frame of mind about receiving instruction and have the incentive to do well in their educational programme. Two possible design models for pre-service are possible:

1 Providing the treatment as a separate course or group of courses and
2 Providing the treatment as an integral part of existing courses.

The choice here may be a very practical one depending on the extent of control, power, or influence that the designer of the intervention has within the particular educational institution or system. The design of a separate course to sensitize teachers in training to sex stereotyping in educational materials and/or in the classroom is probably easier to implement than negotiating with a number of other faculties to have a component that they did not design introduced into their courses and then training these faculty members to use this component.

The in-service programmes for teachers normally function through the use of conferences, workshops, or some other type of training programme. Major problems here are attracting the right people to participate in this training and ensuring the acceptance of what is presented. As Havelock (1973) has described in his model for educational change, opinion leaders, those in formal authority, and those who are the 'gatekeepers' must be involved if the programme is to be creditable and respectable. In addition, the relationship of the school to the larger community must be considered and ways of dealing with the social norms of the community should be incorporated into the programme.

Table 13(1) gives a brief description of a few of the in-service and pre-service teacher-training projects that have been funded under WEEA. In *Tables 13(2)* and *13(3)*, some representative programmes in educational leadership and career preparation are summarized.

Each of these and of the other WEEA projects is required to be 'capacity building'. By this the writers of the regulations meant that the projects would produce materials that could be used by other organizations, agencies, and individuals. The purpose of this requirement is to create as much national impact as possible from these activities. Thus, you will find that, in many of these projects, instructional modules or handbooks are being developed and evaluated. Similarly, many of the training sessions or workshops focus not only on giving the individuals attending new skills to combat sexism in education but also in training them to help others to acquire these skills, or to be resources and change agents in their school or area.

A final need in designing these kinds of intervention is to develop means for others who have similar interests to learn from the projects what is available for their own situation and use. The *Women's Educational Equity Act* programme has asked for the design of a communications network dealing with all topics relevant to women's educational equity. This network, which should be operational some time in 1978, will make it possible for practitioner and researcher alike to identify and acquire all kinds and types of research and development that are being done in this area. Providing such help and service will speed up the process of diffusion and make it possible for the goal of educational equity for all women to be achieved in the near future.

Table 13(1) *Representative teacher-training projects to combat sexism in education*

Pre-service training

Dr Patricia Campbell
Georgia State University
Atlanta, Georgia 30303

Modules on sex roles and stereotyping for the training of elementary and secondary school teachers; to accompany existing courses in such topics as Human Growth and Development, Educational History, etc.

Dr Walter S. Smith
University of Kansas
School of Education
Lawrence, Kansas 66045

Modules for elementary school teachers focussing on the behaviour and attitudes of teachers, sex-role stereotyping awareness, and instructing teachers on how to combat problems of sex-role stereotyping (can also be used for in-service training).

In-service training

Dr Isabel Pico de Hernandez
Commission for the Betterment of Women's Rights
P.O. Box 11382, Fernandez Junco Station
Santurce, Puerto Rico 00910

Materials to develop teacher awareness of the sex biases in Spanish language elementary school reading instruction materials (may also be used for pre-service training).

Dr Marlaine E. Lockheed
Educational Testing Service
Princeton, New Jersey 08541

Teacher training to promote equal status behaviour between boys and girls in grades 4, 5 and 6.

225

Ms Anne Grant WNYE-TV 112 Tillary Street Brooklyn, New York 11201	Seven half-hour television programmes to illustrate current inequitable practices in elementary and secondary education and to demonstrate bias-free alternatives. Workshops to help teachers to use these programmes and serve as change agents in their individual schools.

Table 13(2) *Representative projects for improving educational leadership*

Ms Marjorie Parks George Washington University 2130 H Street, NW Washington, DC 20052	A model training programme for college and university administrators and counsellors on how to develop and administer continuing education for women programmes in their institution. Programme uses a training workshop and provides an administrator's handbook.
Dr Jack Culbertson University Council for Educational Administration 29 West Woodruff Avenue Columbus, Ohio 43210	Uses multi-media instructional modules for in-service training of administrators, policy makers, professors, and graduate students. Deals with inequities in educational opportunities for women.
Dr Sharon Lord University of Tennessee	Programme to train graduate students to provide sex-fair

Department of Educational Psychology
Knoxville, Tennessee 37916

leadership in counselling, careers education, and educational psychology. Uses regional conferences and workshops; provides course modules and an implementation handbook.

Table 13(3) *Representative programmes to improve career preparation*

Dr Lenore Blum
Mills College
Department of Mathematics
Oaklands, California 94613

Restructuring a college's curriculum and career development services to help undergraduates acquire the ability to use mathematics and computer science.

Ms Sallie O'Neill
UCLA University Extension and Human Development Services
10995 LeConte Avenue
Los Angeles, California 90024

Through a five-day residential institute, training higher education and community personnel in group counselling for women and as trainers of paraprofessionals in their area.

Dr L. Sunny Hansen
University of Minnesota
Psychoeducational Studies
Minneapolis, Minnesota 55455

Training modules to assist teachers, parents, counsellors, and teacher and counsellor educators become facilitators of change in career related sex-role stereotyping.

Dr Vera Norwood
New Mexico Commission on the Status of Women
600 2nd NW
Albuquerque, New Mexico 87102

A course on employment awareness to assist entry or re-entry of mature women (age twenty-five to sixty) into the work force.

References

EIBEN, R. and MILLIREN, A. (eds) (1976) *Educational Change: A Humanistic Approach*. La Jolla, Calif.: University Associates, Inc.

EKSTROM, R.B. (1972) *Barriers to Women's Participation in Post-Secondary Education* (RB-72-49). Princeton, N.J.: Educational Testing Service.

FEDERATION OF ORGANIZATIONS FOR PROFESSIONAL WOMEN (1976) *Effecting Social Change for Women*. Washington, DC: Federation of Organizations for Professional Women.

HAVELOCK, R.G. (1973), *The Change Agent's Guide to Innovation in Education*. Englewood Cliffs, N.J.: Educational Technology Publications.

HOWE, F. (ed.) (1975) *Women and the Power to Change*. New York: McGraw-Hill.

MORRISH, I. (1976) *Aspects of Educational Change*. New York: John Wiley and Sons.

RAMALEY, J.A. (ed.) (1978) *Covert Discrimination and Women in the Sciences*. Boulder, Colorado: Westview Press.

THEODORE, A. (1971) The Professional Woman: Trends and Prospects. In, A. Theodore (ed.), *The Professional Woman*. Cambridge, Mass.: Schenkman Publishing Company.

UNITED STATES OFFICE OF EDUCATION (February 12 1976) Women's Educational Equity Act Program Rules and Regulations, *Federal Register*. Washington, D.C.

Afterword

OONAGH HARTNETT, GILL BODEN,
and MARY FULLER

In organizing this Conference we not only wished to facilitate the exchange of ideas and information among researchers; we also wanted to set up a dialogue between researchers and social policy makers with the object of encouraging discussions of the possible contributions that research in the area of sex roles and sex-role stereotyping might make to the formulation and implementation of social policy. To this end we invited Baroness Lockwood of the Equal Opportunities Commission to address the Conference and we hope that her acceptance of the invitation indicates that social policy makers, and implementers, too, feel that academic research in the area of sex roles holds out the possibility of making a contribution towards the fulfilment of their responsibilities, which adds up to a very difficult and delicate task.

The wide-ranging formal and informal discussion that complemented and supplemented the Conference papers also took up the topic of the relationship between pure and applied research

229

and between research and social policy. The view emerged that, as economic and social conditions form part of the matrix of interacting variables that include sex-role behaviours and perceptions, then, unless future research is linked in some way to action for change in these variables, we were open to the charge of confining ourselves to a 'rear-view mirror' perspective and to *post hoc* explanations. This led to the passing of the following resolution:

> 'This conference urges the Equal Opportunities Commission, the Social Science Research Council, the Schools Council, the British Psychological Society, the British Sociological Association and other relevant funding and professional bodies, to sponsor and encourage research directed towards the reduction of sex-role stereotyping. In our view research should concentrate on strategies for modifying attitudes and changing practice, with a view to facilitating equal opportunity.
>
> We believe that priority should be given to the fields of employment and of education, including curriculum development and second chance education.
>
> We are convinced that this research should not be designed only to obtain descriptions of existing attitudes and behaviour, but should be directed towards programmes of action, intervention and innovation and the monitoring of change.'

Since this Conference took place an innovation has been made in the organization of research funding. Two public bodies, the Equal Opportunities Commission and the Social Science Research Council, the first concerned with monitoring public policy and the second mainly with funding fundamental research, have formed a combined committee for the purpose of funding research that is action oriented. This research is in the area of sex roles, concentrating upon projects that will investigate 'under-achievement' in women. Although the funding available at the moment is relatively small, we feel that this is an important initiative. We regard it as a hopeful sign and look forward to its expansion and to the increase of such initiatives in the future.

The Conference on which this book is based has demonstrated that research on sex roles and sex-role stereotyping can contribute to the content, acquisition, and application of knowledge in

230

stimulating ways that fully justify its growing importance within the behavioural and social sciences.

This is not to claim that there is in existence a body of knowledge that could be called 'Feminist Psychology'. Indeed one might go further and question the value of such labels with their implicit fragmenting of areas of knowledge, especially as there is already an unfortunate trend towards overspecialization and differentiation of language even within disciplines, which hinders communication within and between researchers and practitioners. However, while rejecting any claim to the existence or even the desirability of something called 'Feminist Psychology', we should like to draw attention to advantages that should accrue from the use of feminist perspectives and approaches. Indeed we would suggest that some of these advantages are beginning to emerge already. For instance, while it is still necessary to draw attention to the mistaken practice of generalizing to all persons from data based on males only this criticism is now taken seriously. It is also recognized now that we need many more studies of women and girls in order to gain an adequate knowledge and appreciation of the behaviour of females in their own right and before we can begin to understand how much the sexes may have in common or to what extent, in what ways, under what circumstances, and why the sexes may differ. We are increasingly conscious of the dearth of empirical studies in this area, at least in Britain, and of the pressing need to give attention to the practical problems of applying such research. Yet it must be stressed that the emergence of feminist approaches is still in its infancy. This being so it seems appropriate to speculate about the possible implications of the growth of feminist approaches for the search after and application of knowledge. Even the points already made, relating to over-generalization and selection of population, have in themselves an essential contribution to make to an increase in academic rigour.

No more than can be claimed for any other single approach does a feminist perspective supersede all other outlooks. What we would argue is that feminist perspectives are essential to the adequate definition and attainment of excellence in scientific endeavour. The questioning of accepted conceptualizations about the sexes, such as, for example, the dichotomous nature of masculinity and femininity, is central to feminist perspectives. In many cultures, including our own, masculinity and femininity are used as universal symbols of other dualities: mind-body; passive-active; rational-emotional; subjective-objective; personal-political; and so on. Consequently questioning the duality of masculine and feminine leads inevitably to the questioning of these other taken-for-granted dualities. Since these dualities form the substrata of many of our ways of thinking and acting, this questioning, with its concomitant analysis of sex roles and sex-role stereotyping, is likely to have a profound effect upon the type and content of our abstract categories, upon our explanatory models, and upon the manner in which we pursue and apply knowledge.

Specifically by asserting that the personal is political (an insight that feminism can claim to have originated in this form) and by questioning the mutual exclusivity of the active and passive, feminist approaches increase awareness of the complexity of factors and of the interactions between them that are likely to influence human behaviour. This reinforces the rejection of explanations, models, and theories that do not reflect this complexity, for instance by ignoring the social structure, the environment, or individual attributions of meaning. The adoption of feminist approaches should ensure that the individual and the collectivity are *BOTH* given their due.

Along with others, feminist approaches question the subjective-objective duality. This results in the emergence of subjectivity from the subliminal and in so doing encourages proper acknowledgement of the role of subjectivity in scientific endeavours. One becomes aware of both the researchers' and the 'subjects' definitions of their situation and of their attributions of meaning. While this emergence may cause some discomfort to researchers and readers accustomed to the repression of the subjective, it does allow them to exercise their critical faculties upon crucial factors affecting content. Furthermore, oriented as they are to the solution of both practical social dilemmas and theoretical problems, feminist approaches provide a catalyst for bridging artificial gaps between disciplines and between pure and applied research, while at the same time espousing the search for conceptual distinctions that are finer and more precise than the crude divisions wrought by dualistic thinking.

To sum up, it would be doing an injustice to feminist approaches were they perceived as a polemic limited to the achievement of equality for women within an already given system. These approaches go beyond this. They have a contribution to make to the form that the system itself may take. They have something to say about the making of the rules as well as about obeying them, and something to contribute to the establishment of standards and criteria and to equality of opportunity in attempting to reach them. Feminism is an intellectual, political, and ethical approach that is worthy of consideration for a place among other systems of thought that also attempt to address such problems.

Name index

234

Subject index

240